The Long Journey to Software Valuation

Software as an Asset its risks and rewards

Dwight Olson, CLP emeritus

Contents

Forward

Prior to the 1980's, if you brought up the business of software in conversation, it wasn't long before the discussion got around to the subject of software as an asset. Most everyone agreed that the machine, the hardware, had tangible value. You could see it; you could hold it. Computer hardware had a physical presence. It was a three-dimensional entity. At that time, you could ask, who should care about the asset value of the thing called software? You can't see it; you can't hold it. So, what good is valuing it?

Well, software is the language of the computer. Software is used to express applications, programs, and other information on a computer. The internet is a communication channel made up of a huge amount of software. Software is the thinking or logical language that is used to express an idea and its function. Software is the creative tool for our imagination.

The monetary asset value and risks of software have been the subject of much discussion. How did we get to where the value of an idea expressed as software has value in terms of dollars?

Introduction

Some definitions of software

- Software is anything that is not the physical product, or hardware, but is used with the hardware. From www.dictionary.com
- Software is a collection of data or computer instructions that tell the computer how to work. From en.wikipedia.org/wiki/Software
- Software is machine language instructions, consisting of groups of binary codes for a computer's processing unit. From en.wikipedia.org/wiki/Software
- Software, called firmware, is low-level control for specific hardware such as consumer appliances and medical devices. From en.wikipedia.org/wiki/firmware

Comments by business professionals about software and where

software is used.

"More and more major businesses and industries are being run on software and delivered as online services—from movies to agriculture to national defense. Perhaps the single most dramatic example of this phenomenon of software replacing a traditional business is the collapse of Borders (ed. a traditional 40-year-old book chain that went out of business) and corresponding rise of Amazon."[1]

"Software is like entropy. It is difficult to grasp, weighs nothing, and obeys the second law of thermodynamics; i.e. it always increases."[2]

"It has been said that software is one of the fundamental means by which we innovate. We use it to eliminate jobs and make enterprises more efficient and competitive. It puts greater and greater power into the hands of individuals, so that they can have more power over the means of production. For example, it is said 'Now, you can just get a laptop, get some software, put a microphone on it, and make a record. You must know how to do it. It does help if you've had 35 or 40 years of experience in the studio. But it still levels the playing field so artists can record their own stuff'."[3]

"After all, with a laptop, some software, and a 3D printer, you could be able to manufacture quite complex plastic and

[1] Marc Andreessen, venture capitalist and co-founder of Netscape
[2] Norman Ralph Augustine, former CEO of Lockheed Martin
[3] Roger McGuinn founder, lead singer, and lead guitarist of The Byrds

metal goods on your own. And all because of some very sophisticated modeling and design software, a high-speed processor, and 3D printing technology."[4]

"The internet and software resources can be put in the hands of the individual, they are available and economical. No longer is the worker at the mercy of a few rich people holding most of the capital. No longer at the mercy of huge corporations for a job. The creative worker, musician, entrepreneur, software developer, investor, travel agent, industrialist, etc. have the tools to create a living for themselves, and through the internet with software have access to world markets. This software-created revolution in the economic power of the individual is also matched by what software is being made to do for the corporation. Companies' competitiveness has been transformed using:

- software frameworks;
- software modeling, development, and test tools;
- business models built on providing software as a service, or through software applications;
- software systems that manage many of the enterprise's operations processes;
- software collaboration tools that effectively integrate the work of global design and development teams.

Software is eating our traditional businesses, in addition to creating whole new businesses. It is the locus of contemporary capitalism's 'Creative Destruction, a term

---

[4] www.iam-magazine.com

coined by Joseph Schumpter's reading of Karl Marx'[5]. It is how the corporation is innovating, how it does business, how it innovates, and what it is in business to do. In a computer-based company the value is in the software. The software is the product. The product is what you sell or license, and therefore what holds the value for the company. And, application specific devices (such as monitoring systems) are being morphed into software that runs on general purpose computers. Technology trends, marketing competition, and to be financially competitive, are forcing the company's software to be extracted from the company's hardware, and the hardware, for the most part, is being commoditized. The competitive differentiation is in the software."[6]

Bill Elkington[7], an intellectual property professional, has written in the magazine IAM[8],

"The automobile industry is a good example of some of these trends. One reads that 40 percent of the value of a new car today is in its electronic systems. One reads that a typical car has 40 to 50 controllers and microprocessors and that luxury models contain double this number. One reads

---

[5] "Constant revolutionizing of production, uninterrupted disturbance of all social relations, everlasting uncertainty and agitation, distinguish the bourgeois epoch from all earlier times. All fixed, fast-frozen relationships, with their train of venerable ideas and opinions, are swept away, all new-formed ones become obsolete before they can ossify. All that is solid melts into air, all that is holy is profaned, and men at last are forced to face with sober senses the real conditions of their lives and their relations with their fellow men."

[6] www.iam-magazine.com

[7] Bill Elkington, Past-President, Licensing Executives Society, worked at Rockwell Collins where he provided leadership in multiple dimensions of IP management.

[8] Intellectual Asset Management (www.iam-magazine.com)

that a typical new car today runs about 10 million lines of computer code, with projections as high as 30 times that number in about 10 years, to accommodate the greater and greater automation of the car's various systems, reaching substantially into the complete operation of the automobile itself—the 'driver-less car' that Google and others are promoting."

There are many financing reasons to value software (See Exhibit F for a description of each), for example to name a few:

- Acquisition Financing
- Debt Financing
- Business Sale/Purchase
- Management Stewardship
- Intercompany Transfer Pricing
- Gifting Programs
- Estate Planning

Chapter 1

How did software become an asset? Setting the course.

Before 1976 mainframe computer manufactures included software as part of the computer mainframe deliverables at no charge. Software was free, that is, there was no charge for the software that was included to make the computer operate. The free software usually included an operating system[9], assemblers[10], file management[11], and language compilers[12]. In 1976 International Business Machines[13] (IBM) unbundled the software from the hardware and began to charge a royalty license for the software.

---

[9] An operating system (OS) is software that manages the interaction between hardware resources and the programs or applications you use on a computer.
[10] a computer program which translates assembly language to machine language.
[11] a computer program that provides a user interface to manage files.
[12] a computer program that translates computer code written in a programming language into machine code (for the target computer)
[13] See https://en.wikipedia.org/wiki/IBM

Most mainframe[14] computer manufactures followed suit. This was earth-shattering within the industry as both computer manufacturing companies and buyers had to learn new rules of licensing and acquiring software independently of the hardware. This opened the door for software entrepreneurs and new software companies to offer additional software product options to the hardware manufactures software including computer 'software tools and applications'[15].

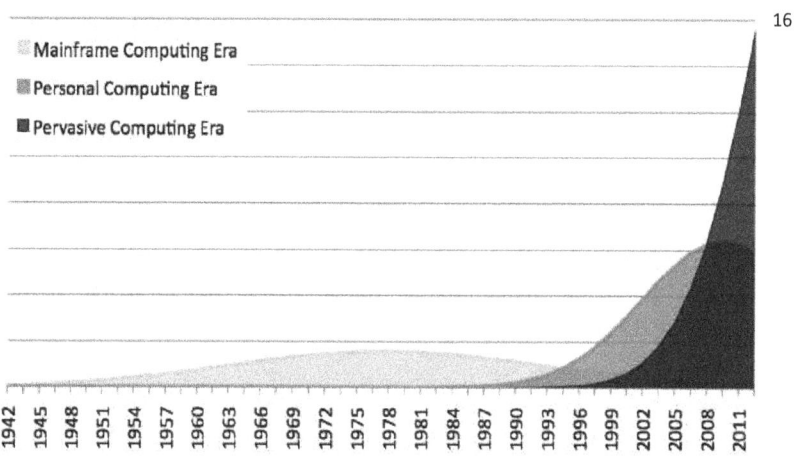

---

[14] The term originally referred to the large cabinets called "main frames" that housed the central processing unit and main memory of early computers.

[15] A software tool is a computer program that software developers use to create, debug, maintain, or otherwise support other programs and applications. The most basic tools are a source code editor and a compiler or interpreter, which are used ubiquitously and continuously. The distinction between tools and applications is murky. For example, developers use simple databases (such as a file containing a list of important values) all the time as tools. See Wikipedia software tools.

[16] Müller, Jörg & Alt, Florian & Michelis, Daniel. (2011). Pervasive Advertising. 10.1007/978-0-85729-352-7_1.

Prior to the 1980's a serious issue for all software development was that all investments in software were immediately expensed, as opposed to hardware development. Hardware development could be capitalized. Capitalized costs arise in relation to the research and development of computer hardware, where some costs can be capitalized. Capitalized costs are depreciated or amortized over multiple years. Thus, capitalization is used to recognize a cash outlay as an asset on the balance sheet, rather than an expense on the income statement. This meant for computer manufacturing companies, hardware research and development investments did not immediately appear on the expense line, but investments in software did. Thus, companies with hardware and software development had corporate book values that were somewhat distorted. Because of this distortion, at Control Data Corporation[17], for instance, management directives from their upper management, were to minimize software investments. This distortion possibly caused other mainframe manufactures to also cut back in the development of software for their equipment.

As miniaturization of the computer hardware from mainframe to personal computer was occurring over the 1980's, most computer manufactures could no longer supply sufficient software for the needs of their market. With an increasing demand for application and tools software for all types of computers, from mainframe, mini-computers, to microcomputers there was a growing void for software in the marketplace. This void helped to open the market

---

[17] Control Data Corporation (CDC) was a mainframe and supercomputer firm. CDC was one of the nine major United States computer companies through most of the 1960s; the others were IBM, Burroughs Corporation, DEC, NCR, General Electric, Honeywell, RCA, and UNIVAC. CDC was well-known and highly regarded throughout the industry at the time. For most of the 1960s, Seymour Cray worked at CDC and developed a series of machines that were the fastest computers in the world.

for even more independent software companies to start-up, grow and supply software products, not only directly to computer manufactures, like Microsoft's MS-DOS[18], but more importantly to their clients.

As more and more software companies appeared during the 1980's, they too wanted to know more about how software could be an asset. Their financial officers' ask questions;

- can software development also be capitalized,
- is software valued like physical assets,
- is software protectable as intellectual property,

But, software as an asset brought risk questions:

- Who owns the rights to make money from the software, the company or someone else?
- Can software assets help increase company's net worth?
- Can software assets be used in an IPO?
- Can an institution lend to a company based on its software assets as its collateral?
- What instruments mitigate risk of software as an asset?

Companies who were licensing software products knew that the inherent value of their software increased as factors of market potential polarized. Intellectual property advocates knew that software with rights to license also contributed to increased

---

[18] MS-DOS is an operating system for x86-based personal computers mostly developed by Microsoft. Collectively, MS-DOS, its rebranding as IBM PC DOS, and some operating systems attempting to be compatible with MS-DOS, are sometimes referred to as "DOS" (which is also the generic acronym for disk operating system).

revenue opportunities. Plus, revenue forecasting for software also began to take shape when the company had the resources necessary to prepare for market and sales. These factors were not monetary or earnings values, they were factors that revealed the inherent value of the software product.

Software began the asset journey when corporations that were developing software products for the computer marketplace wanted to capitalize their software development investments, much like their hardware counterparts, but couldn't, due to federal regulations. They needed to get approval from the US's Federal Accounting Standards Board (FASB).

Thus, an 'Issues Paper' on software as an asset was prepared by the AICPA[19]'s Accounting Standards Division's task force. The task force included members of ADAPSO—the Computer Software and Services Industry Association (formerly known as the Association of Data Processing Service Organizations) and the National Association of Accountants. The 'Issues Paper' was titled "Accounting for Costs of Software for Sale or Lease". The 'Issues Paper' recommended that certain costs incurred in creating computer software for sale or lease, be recorded as an asset if the software met certain conditions relating to market, technology, financial and management. In February 1984, FASB received the 'Issues Paper' from the AICPA.

On August 31, 1984, FASB released an 'Exposure Draft' for public comment on the accounting for the costs of computer software to

---

[19] American Institute of Certified Public Accountants (AICPA) is the national professional organization of Certified Public Accountants (CPAs) in the United States, with more than 418,000 members in 143 countries in business and industry, public practice, government, education, student affiliates and international associates.

be sold, leased, or otherwise marketed as a separate software product or as part of a product/process. The 'Exposure Draft' proposed that the costs incurred internally in creating a computer software product, would be charged to expense until cost recoverability had been established by determining the software product feasibility of:

- market,
- technology viable,
- financial viability for the product and
- management had or could obtain the resources to produce and market the product and was committed to doing so.

The 'Exposure Draft' meant the costs of the detail program design components were to be charged to expense, and the costs of producing the product inventory masters, including coding and testing, were to be capitalized. The capitalized costs would be reviewed periodically for recoverability. All costs of planning, designing, and establishing the technological feasibility of a computer software product would be the research and development costs.

After the public comment period, FASB issued a final statement on software accountability (See Exhibit E) on August 8, 1985. This would be the first-time software could appear on the financial books of a company. We now had the road for the journey of software as an asset with value. However, FASB reached somewhat different conclusions from the recommendations in the 'Issues Paper', they were more lenient.

FASB No. 86 Statement[20] specified that costs incurred internally in creating software product components should be charged to expense when incurred as research and development until only technological feasibility has been established for the product. Technological feasibility was established upon completion of a detail program design[21] or, in its absence, completion of a working model. That is, planning, designing, coding, and lab testing activities that are necessary to establish that the software can meet its design specifications, including functions, features, and performance requirements. This perspective on technology feasibility gives us some basis of value, especially for people who wish to immediately 'monetize'[22]. Technology that has a working model has less risk and more potential for value than technology that does not have a working model. This may be intuitive, but important to state especially when the software exists in some forms and works.

I want to cover in more detail the other factors that were considered important by the software industry as indicators of value. They are value factor propositions of:
- intellectual property (IP)
- management
- market

---

[20] See https://www.fasb.org/pdf/fas86.pdf
[21] From Wikipedia "A software design description (SDD) is a written description of a software product, that a software designer writes in order to give a software development team overall guidance to the architecture of the software project. An SDD usually accompanies an architecture diagram with pointers to detailed feature specifications of smaller pieces of the design. Practically, the description is required to coordinate a large team under a single vision, needs to be a stable reference, and outline all parts of the software and how they will work."
[22] Such as license patent(s) prior to commercialization, or even sell their rights in the software.

- financial feasibility

The intellectual property factors.

Those in the software product licensing business know that certain intellectual property requirements must in place:
- work for hire assignments to the company,
- freedom to commercialize investigated,
- intellectual property protections, and
- encumbrance considerations documented.

Patents and trademarks can be intellectual property protections for a software product. I consider them as software product 'inventory components' (more on this later), and are legal protections for disclosure of certain software product inventory components released to the public. Copyright, patent, and trademark also provide the legal framework for software product licensing. Understanding the intellectual property rights and ownership aspects of software are critically important for the ability to create and maintain revenue. Without having the intellectual property protections and rights in place for the software it may not create licensing revenue.

Software business professionals know that in the early stages of software product development, copyright and patent assignments of ownership, freedom to commercialize, and securing intellectual property rights needs to be done. Identifying and securing intellectual property also means understanding who also has intellectual property in the area of commercialization. For example, before filing for patent protection, a comprehensive literature search needs to be carried out on a global basis, to identify any prior art, or published information related to the idea and area of interest. These searches also will help in preparing the initial business plan for the start of commercialization.

Even if there are no patent considerations, prior art searches for market information will reveal which companies are active in the area of the software product. This is particularly important since this identifies potential licensees. The searches also provide the benefit of knowing who the competition might be. The search may also locate companies and individuals to contact to get marketing information about the areas of interest. A final point on doing detailed intellectual property background research, is that the telephone is still a useful and efficient way to get information. Good market information can be obtained by simply asking the right question.

It is obvious that an issued patent or patent application embodying or relating to the technology will potentially increase the commercial desirability of the software product, assuming the patent claims embody the technology. Intellectual property discussions and research for other software product protections must also be done for trademarks, and copyrights. A discussion regarding the risk and use of open source software[23] is extremely important at this stage. An initial discussion of open source is in Chapter 10.

The management commitment factor.

In consideration of software as a capital asset, the 'Exposure Draft'

---

[23] See https://www.synopsys.com/ - Open Source Security and Risk Analysis (OSSRA) Report

considered management commitment an important requirement. The 'Exposure Draft' proposed that the costs incurred internally in creating a computer software product would be charged to expense until cost recoverability had been established by determining ... and "management had or could obtain the resources to produce and market the product and was committed to doing so."

An important part of the management factor is the existence of a business plan with both a marketing 'strategy' and a marketing 'operational' section for making money with the software product. The business plan is the 'rallying cry' of any start-up venture. It should be considered by anyone thinking of monetizing[24] a component of the asset inventory such as the patent. The business plan should be considered as one of the components of the software inventory.

With sound management in place, the business plan helps angel[25] investors understand potential value and initial guidance. The business plan also acts as the operations manual for the development of the software product's inventory components and can act as a reference tool for management. It's therefore very crucial to think through the early stages of development with a sound business plan for discussion of getting additional financial commitments for the initial market entry and capital requirement during its life cycle.

In developing the business plan, one should analyze strengths,

---

[24] Monetizing is used here to mean the immediate sale or license of all or part of the existing innovative stage software product components.
[25] refers to anyone who invests his or her money in an entrepreneurial company (unlike institutional venture capitalists, who invest other people's money).

weaknesses, opportunities, and threats. An effective business plan should:

1. help focus ideas about a market opportunity and how to turn them into a realistic course of action,
2. create a path to follow in the years of diffusion of the product,
3. identify milestones & benchmarks that can measure progress,
4. be succinct, interesting, and sufficiently solid enough to attract prospective investors, buyers, or licensees, and
5. be thoughtful and flexible enough to handle contingencies and unexpected events.

If one is looking to find institutional investors in the commercialization phases (diffusion stage), then one must keep in mind what institutional investors are looking for:

- a specific and realistic source of value that differentially fulfills a specific and unmet need,
- a management team that can plan and execute the business plan with success, and
- of course, a sustainable and defensible product/service position.

The risk, usefulness, and 'value' of the business plan to make money will be evaluated by all investors for soundness and appropriateness. Institutional investors will of course focus primarily on the financial section, but a sensible business plan will be a requirement to getting investments.

Some thoughts on the market factors.

A major cause of failure of any innovation usually relates to market analysis. The truth about innovation is most ideas or inventions never make it to commercialization. For example, it has been estimated that only 5% of active patents are being commercially utilized. Some studies have also shown that only one idea is commercialized out of 1000 new ideas and that only 1 in 4 products in development get commercialized. Why are there so many failures? Dr. Robert Cooper[26] a pioneer in new product development processes, investigated a cause of failure of new ideas at many companies. He concluded the major cause of failure relates to market analysis. That is, the companies did not understand their target markets well enough to know how to market properly or whether they should even have been committed to commercialization at all.

A section of the business plan should address market feasibility. Why would someone buy or license the software product? Some issues involved in market analysis consider market size and growth, today and in the future. It will be important to know target customers and ways in which to capitalize on them in order to bring additional profitability and lasting sustainability.

If the ultimate product or service is new, market research will put meaningful dimensions on the initial business plan and the market. If the product or service represents an improvement on what is available, there may already be well-defined dimensions to the market. In the market analysis it is important to show historical data and reliable forecasts from industry, trade associations or government sources and provide answers for questions such as;

---

[26] see also Winning-New-Products-Creating-Innovation

- Who are the customers?
- What is the historic and predicted rate of growth for each market segment?
- Where are the present and future markets? Are they regional, national, or international?
- How does each market segment purchase the product?
- What are the critical characteristics?
- What substitutes are available for this product?
- Does the market have any special characteristics, such as a seasonal factor?

If the technology is new, one may likely face entrenched competition from mature organizations with far greater resources. Identify competitors in the business plan and note their strengths, weaknesses and market share of each. Be realistic about the analysis and address all the negatives to show that commercialization is possible for the software product. The business plan should also indicate the market share expected in the first three to five years. In the plan, cite the principal competitive factors in the marketplace: product performance, reliability, durability, styling, delivery, service, aggressive merchandising, and price. Identify trends with an explanation of how to react to them. An initial prospective investor will want to know how competitors are likely to react to entry into the market of the software product and how to respond. Perhaps the greatest temptation will be to overstate the technology strengths and understate competitors' weaknesses and skills.

The marketing section is a crucial element of the business plan, and its importance is often underestimated. It should define market strategy as well as operational (tactical) strategy that charts the direction for the marketing staff. Investors want reassurance that the technology could generate a growing profit stream. The marketing section of the business plan normally contains a detailed initial marketing strategy for market entry of the software product. Regardless of whether the software technology is in the innovation stage or syndication stage the plan should summarize the marketing goals. The goals should be quantitative, realistic and consistent with the financial analysis.

The business plan should address how to price the software product compared to the competition. The plan should support that price by identifying ways in which the software product adds value if there are readily available substitutes in the market for the product.   As pricing may change at different times in commercialization, the plan should address how competition might react.

The business plan should address strategy for building sales and therefore revenues. The plan should be consistent with both market data and financial projections. Advertising on the internet, email campaigns, as well as traditional media such as television commercials must all come under consideration. The market must be aware of the brand and want to choose the product, given that there is a need. The plan should address how much of the promotion will be handled internally and how much will be outsourced. If the marketing team has been selected prior to the diffusion stage the investors will want to know who they are.

As mentioned, the business plan is an important part of the software product inventory. The efforts and money expended in the early stages of development of the product's business plan should be considered to add value to the software product. If the business plan does not address the considerations outlined in this section, the software may not be financed.

The financial factor.

The pre-FASB No. 86 Software 'Exposure Draft' proposed that the costs incurred internally in creating a computer software product would be charged to expense until cost recoverability had been established by determining financial feasibility for the product. Simply put, the software product would make money.

The financial section of the business plan contains the monetary forecasting of revenue. This section is the most difficult for nearly anyone. In some ways this will be the gem for the software product and may be the only factor considered by additional investors. The forecasting of potential revenues, expenses and profits are not the easiest of tasks. A financial plan should contain a discussion of the costs, revenue and potential earnings associated with the software product and services in the diffusion stage. It is sometimes very easy to associate a market share or royalty rate with an existing market share. For example, in pharmaceuticals there is a lot of data available about sales from the date of introduction showing how quickly a drug can be ramped up and where it peaks. If there is a new drug in a similar category and it has an advantage, like elimination of a side effect, there is guidance for forecasting the new and better drug. This might be helpful if the software is associated with a device or drug in the pharmaceutical industry.

Data can be found for blockbuster add-on products like cell phones, DVDs, and other associated products showing where there might be a rapid climb in sales. But what about some university or entrepreneur that invents some sort of new and fantastic 3D generation of a shoe insert, or some other unknown? This is where the difficult financial analysis will be. In licensing software, the transfer rights may include exclusive or nonexclusive rights to specified software inventory components, patents, technical data, rights to future improvements, rights to sublicense, installation, user documentation, support for problems and bug fixes, future updates and the like. These items need to be considered in setting any price and will impact the financial projections.

In the year 2000, many considered that we were at the beginning of an era that would consider wealth of this new information age to be the technology patent assets. These assets are of importance to governments, organization, and the global public. However, as we progress into the 21st century, we need to update this consideration to include all software product inventory assets. If so, then wealth in the 21st century will be measured in the ownership, licensing, commercialization and management of all intellectual assets.

Two thoughts on software asset value. The first is from the book *Valuing Your Business For An Investor*, 2002, by D.W.Berkus who writes,

> "There is an eleventh method – but it is one I use only as a rule of thumb to size up the first ten. For early stage companies, I use the "Berkus Method" approach. I give $500,000 valuation credit for the attractiveness of the core idea upon which the company is founded (if I am attracted to it). I add another $500,000 if I believe good management is already in place to execute to the plan in the early stages of rapid growth. Then I add $500,000 if the company has struck impressive strategic alliances with either vendors or customers, adding to barriers of entry for other businesses.

Finally, I add $500,000 if the company has completed its product or prototype and demonstrated its attractiveness before an appreciative customer candidate, which all goes to further reduce the risk of investment, adding to value."

The second thought is from a book by John Ramsay, a close Licensing Executive Society friend, *Ramsay on Technology Transfer*, 3d edition, writes,

"There is no one 'right way' to value technology. Whatever the purpose, the valuation will involve a risk/benefit assessment by the parties involved. Although evaluation may have objective tools available, they will ultimately have to subjectively assess the importance of the various objective factors to the party to the transaction performing the valuation."

By the year 2000 we knew that the information age was here, and we saw an increasing number of corporations accumulating wealth based on software. We watched Microsoft's enterprise value in the year 2000 pass one quarter of a trillion dollars with annual revenue exceeding twenty billion dollars, with much of it due to software licensing. In 2020 Microsoft value hit one trillion dollars in corporate value. Yet, even today, how many line items on corporate financials are touting ownership of software assets.

The journey has started, but one is still left with the thought "where's the beef"?

Chapter 2

The Software valuation journey begins.

As pointed out earlier, software can be as simple as information covering a color scheme for a package, or a client list. Software can be as complex as millions of lines of source code for a computer operating system, a huge 3D bio-database, a massively scalable online financial system. Software can also be as subtle as the process sequence of certain pharmaceutical manufacturing steps. Software is even firmware driving a logic chip's[27] control of a medical device. Software often makes a huge difference between success or failure for a corporation.

---

[27] a processor or controller "logic chip" in which fixed operations are performed

Some definitions will be helpful in reading this book:

- **R&D** – Research and development (R&D) – is the process by which a company works to obtain new knowledge that it might use to create new technology, products, or services that it will either use or sell.
- **Source code** - Source code is the human-readable statements of computer programming.
- **Source code comments** - In computer programming, a comment is a programmer-readable explanation or annotation in the source code of a computer program. They are added with the purpose of making the source code easier for humans to understand.
- **Software development tools** – A set of software development tools such as compilers, assemblers, and other system software.
- **Object code** - A form of software that can be run in the computer. For example, a computer-based programming language compiler called C++[28] translates source code into computer-readable code called object code.
- **Build guides** - Build guides are the instructions to software tools that prepare an executable. Software build is also referred to for the process of converting source code files into object code files. Object code files along with 3rd party software (software created by independent programmers or publishers) are collected into an 'executable' application that can be run on a computer.
- **System software** - System software is software designed to provide a platform for other software. Examples of system

---

[28] A C++ compiler is itself a computer program who's only job is to convert the C++ program from source code form to a form the computer can read and execute.

software include operating systems like Unix, macOS, Linux OS and Microsoft Windows. In contrast to system software, software that allows users to do user-oriented tasks such as create text documents, play games, listen to music, or browse the web are collectively referred to as application software. If we think of the computer system as a layered model, the system software is the interface between the hardware and user applications. The operating system is the best-known example of system software.

The life of a software product is in four stages[29]:

- **Innovation stage**: This stage represents the building of enough software inventory components for alpha testing[30] of the software.
- **Syndication stage**: This stage represents the building of all remaining software inventory components required for commercialization. The software has become a product. (See Typical Software Product Inventory Assets below).
- **Diffusion stage**: This stage represents the licensing (sales) and market penetration of the software product.
- **Substitution stage**: This last stage represents decline or the need for update/replacement of the software product.

A software product's typical inventory asset components.

---

[29] See also https://techliebe.com/do-you-know-what-is-product-life-cycle/
[30] to simulate the real user by using simulation techniques. It is carried out with in a lab-environment.

Typical Software Product Inventory Assets
Disclosed inventory assets
• Software program for user – usually in executable format
• User documentation (paper and digital)
• Access to support FAQ's
• Patents and trademarks
Undisclosed inventory assets
• R&D components (e.g. internal design documentation)
• Installation and training documentation
• Program source code with comments
• Source code control system documentation with comments
• Various databases (e.g. error corrections, licensing data)
• Error and Bug support systems
• Client support and billing
• Testing code
• 3rd party software and licenses
• Open source software and guides
• Quality assurance data and processes
• System software with software tools database
• Specific build guides for program deliverables
• Program support documents
• Software enhancement plans
• Business plans (with marketing plans)

At the end of the syndication stage, some undisclosed software inventory assets are used to 'build' or 'software manufacture' a specific software product's disclosed inventory. Some disclosed components are typically trademarked and known as the released software product. The disclosed inventory or 'specific' software product is now available to the introduction cycle of the diffusion stage.

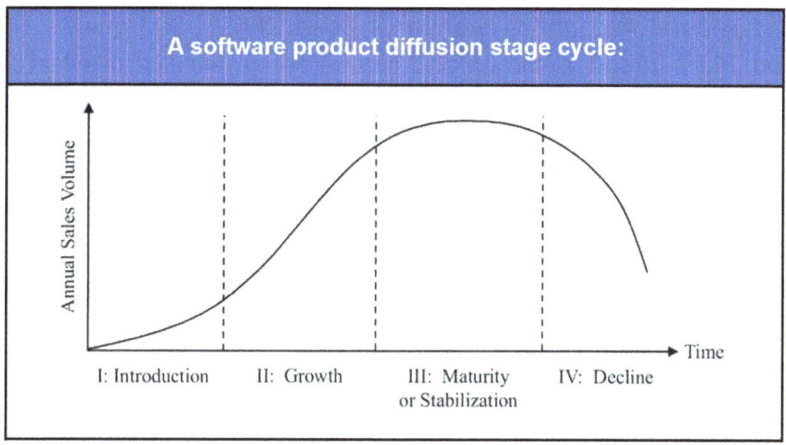

So, how do companies get management and financial control around software as an asset? If we consider the costs of only those companies that just build software used only internally to harness some aspect of their business, be it methods to schedule their services more effectively, or adding additional capabilities to their tangible products they deliver, then we are encompassing an enormous number of companies from startups to Fortune 100's. The amount of money invested by these companies is in the mega billions. A 2004 report, based on a survey of 226 top professionals from many industries, revealed that more than 75% of respondents reported their businesses were dependent on information technology[31] (IT), and that nearly 50% of all capital expenditures were spent on IT.[32] As well, nearly 70% of respondents report an inability to compute return on investment for software capital goods and typical lifetimes of information systems that have an average life of over twenty years.

As early as 2002 government regulations such as Sarbanes-Oxley[33] and Federal Accounting Standards Board (FASB) Statements 141 and 142[34] forced valuation and careful governance of intellectual assets including software. Probes for transparency to understand a corporation's intellectual assets and how they are used, are changing both the governance of software assets and their financial importance. Governments want to be able to tax appropriately; stockholders want management to maximize value, and the financial world wants to have a more knowable investment in a digital company and its future.

---

[31] Information technology is the technology involving the development, maintenance, and use of computer systems, software, and networks for the processing and distribution of data.

[32] See BPM Forum, December 2004

[33] The Sarbanes–Oxley Act of 2002, enacted July 30, 2002), (SOX) also known as the "Public Company Accounting Reform and Investor Protection Act" and "Corporate and Auditing Accountability, Responsibility, and Transparency Act" and more commonly called Sarbanes–Oxley , is a United States federal law that set new or expanded requirements for all U.S. public company boards, management and public accounting firms.

[34] Corporations that have completed a merger and acquisition (M&A) transaction since June 30, 2001, have had to comply with the valuation and accounting provisions of Statements of Financial Accounting Standards (SFAS) No. 141, Business Combinations, and No. 142, Goodwill and Other Intangibles. These Financial Accounting Standards Board (FASB) statements establish generally accepted accounting principles (GAAP) for M&A financial accounting. In most M&A transactions, SFAS No. 141 and 142 affects both the accounting for and the valuation of the acquired company assets, and particularly the acquired goodwill.

How did those in post-modern corporations' value intellectual property (IP) or provide expert guidance on patent risk? Did they do any software inventory valuation apart from the patent and trademark? If not, how should it be done? Now, in this new information society, how should we think about a software products value contexts and risk management? If software is shared with a business partner, what value should be extract and what risk mitigation performed? Are the value contexts of the other components of software as problematic as that of software patents[35]? Is there something to a software product that one can get their arms around? Is the software product somehow more substantive? More understandable? More comprehensible? Is its value more demonstrative? More objectively derivable?

In a company's merger or acquisition, there is found a broad range of intellectual assets in the form of intellectual property and intangibles including software. How does a software product affect a merger whether it is licensed in, out, or just used internally? The FASB 141/142 rules in a purchase price allocation calls for a valuation house to identify all intangible assets including software with definable lives, and to then depreciate these assets over the remaining useful life.

Raz Razgaitis writes about valuation of technology that also applies to software,

> "The value of a technology to a buyer (or licensee) depends upon how it is to be commercially employed, considering the cost of development and commercialization, the time the technology takes to generate returns, the extent of

---

[35] See www.forbes.com on the-problems-with-software-patents

such financial returns, and the risk involved in the process. At the time of a licensing/sale transaction of technology many, perhaps all, of such factors need to be assessed and quantified by making judgments about how the future will unfold with respect to the technology being developed. This assessment and forecast assessment are the essence of all pro forma business models. Valuing license rights for early-stage technologies is in this sense no different than making other future business forecasts, though the details may differ because the forecast time horizon may be longer, the uncertainties may be greater as to the market size and profitability, the operating performance of the technology as it will be used in commercial operation may be less well defined. The price paid for a technology transferred between parties is the amount of money (present and future) and/or the financial value of noncash assets given in exchange for the transfer of the technology, which can only occur if both the seller (licensor) and buyer (licensee) have by some process reached a common, present understanding of value that makes agreement possible."[36]

At the beginning of the 21st century, accurately identifying, analyzing, and evaluating, software by and within an enterprise became important, and ever more critical was the concern for software asset valuation and software asset risk management. Management of risk and financial controls began with understanding what were the software product inventory components. These are the typical components required to bring a

---

[36] Pricing the Intellectual Property of Early-Stage Technologies: A Primer of Basic Valuation, RICHARD RAZGAITIS, Senior Advisor, CRA International, Inc., U.S.A.

software product to market.

In the development of the software inventory assets, knowing what factors impact the ability to make money with the inventory is important. Knowing what the value is for owning all the inventory and the management of the risks associated with the components is also important. Managing the risks and owning all the inventory assets is called the total software value of the software product. Getting one's arms around the value contexts and the risk management of all component assets are sometimes most difficult.

How does one value a software product apart from its inventory components of patent and trademark? Much is written about patent and trademark valuation, but what about other software inventory components? Most patent and trademark valuation discussions deal with infringement by another party and not specifically with the concept of ownership of the patent or trademark inventory components. The terms "stick licensing and carrot licensing"[37] are quite commonly used and discussed in patent and trademark valuations. Today, the value of the software product is not just held in any patents or trademarks that protect the embodiment of the software product deliverables. In my opinion, it is even more than the licensing revenue of the software product; it can be much more. Many of these inventory components, are 'trade secrets'[38] and where the real value may be.

---

[37] Wiki - Stick licensing is the practice of licensing a patent or other form of intellectual property where the patent holder threatens to sue the licensee for patent infringement if the licensee does not take a license. In contrast to the stick licensing, the "carrot licensing" is a "friendly approach in luring the target to adopting one's invention and taking a license"

[38] The Uniform Trade Secret Act defines a "trade secret" as: "information, including a

The intellectual assets owned by any development enterprise, include: the technical knowledge (or know-how) of its staff, the competence of its sales force, the business knowledge (experience) of its management, its goodwill and reputation, the commercial value of its licenses, and the value of its software inventory. Mr. Kemerer, a writer for InformationWeek[39] wrote,

> "Do you know what your software inventory is worth? It's a question you may not have heard, or even thought of, but knowing the value of your software inventory can help you manage it better."[40]

Valuation and risk management are not easy tasks as many software products are complex systems that involve many inventory components, networks and 3rd party software including open source. Many software products are highly sophisticated, and highly integrated. Many software products cost millions of dollars to develop, millions of dollars to deploy, and tens of millions of dollars to adapt to ever-shifting conditions over time.

In this information age, purchasing, licensing or developing complex technology, companies just look at the total cost of the

---

formula, pattern, compilation, program, device, method, technique, or process that: derives independent economic value, actual or potential, from not being generally known to, and not being readily ascertainable by proper means by, other persons who can obtain economic value from its disclosure or use; and Is the subject of efforts that are reasonable under the circumstances to maintain its secrecy.

[39] InformationWeek defines the value of technology in the age of digital business. As the world's most trusted business technology resource, InformationWeek offers independent insight and advice to help today's IT leaders navigate the fast-changing technology landscape and identify the best strategies and tools to drive their organizations forward. See www.informationweek.com

[40] Value your App Inventory, Chris F. Kemerer, InformationWeek of May 25, 1998

project, which consists of hardware, software and associated services. It is important to remember that software obsolescence is not tied to specific computer hardware, software can typically be upgraded to new computer hardware. For example, Unix[41] (trademarked as UNIX) is a family of multitasking, multiuser computer operating systems that derive from the original AT&T UNIX, with development in the 1970s at the Bell Labs research center. Unix variants exist in forms today, Wikipedia lists over 40 from Aix to Xenix.

Using a software product's potential license revenue to compute a fair value[42] (such as using a net present value[43] (NPV) calculation) for the entire software product is not an easy task. There are many reasons for this such as questionable forecasting and the inability to associate revenue streams back to the various software inventory components. One solution for many of the inventory components is to do a cost analysis using the replacement method. A cost-based valuation model focuses on the costs incurred to develop the software component. It provides an estimate for the

---

[41] The history of Unix dates back to the mid-1960s when the Massachusetts Institute of Technology, AT&T Bell Labs, and General Electric were jointly developing an experimental time-sharing operating system called Multics for the GE-645 mainframe.

[42] In investing, fair value refers to an asset's sale price agreed upon by a willing buyer and seller. However, in accounting, fair value represents the estimated worth of various assets and liabilities that must be listed on a company's financial statement.

[43] In finance, the net present value (NPV) or net present worth (NPW) applies to a series of cash flows occurring at different times. The present value of a cash flow depends on the interval of time between now and the cash flow. It also depends on the discount rate. NPV accounts for the time value of money. It provides a method for evaluating and comparing capital projects or financial products with cash flows spread over time, as in loans, investments, payouts from insurance contracts plus many other applications.

ownership value[44] of the asset that is tied to the cost to create or acquire the ownership of the inventory asset.

> "This is one of the best ways to create some minimum value, especially for young software companies, or where the investment in technology has been heavy and the life span of the technology is long. Replacement value goes up where there is a high barrier to entry due to proprietary tools, patents, or new technologies. The replacement value assigned to the software is determined by calculating the amount of time and cost which would be saved in the rewrite of the company's products. The value of the installed base may generally be figured at around four times the recurring revenue."[45]

But don't forget the copyright issue for the components:

> "Ownership of the copyright in software source code is important because the copyright owner controls the ability to generate code that can be copied, distributed, and licensed. The owner controls the ability to modify the source code and controls the ability to profit from the new generated code. Under copyright law, the author of a line of software code is the owner of the copyright in that code."[46]

The importance of the intellectual property factors of which ownership is one area to be considered and ownership is a must for

---

[44] Value to owner is the value of a specific item to a particular investor based on an individual investor's requirements and expectations. Valuations performed in pursuance of the value to owner objective consider benefits that arise from the ownership, which motivate retention for an indefinite period. See www.divestopedia.com

[45] https://bridgesdunnrankin.com/valuing-a-software-company/

[46] asp-software.org/www/misv_resources/business-articles/who-owns-the-code/

all inventory components. A note of caution should be taken when open source[47] software is as an inventory component in the software product. See chapters on open source as there are possible issue with patents and certain open source licenses.

In replacement valuations for software products, it is important to remember to identify and cost all software product components using both actual financial costs as well as cost models. Reasonableness[48] equations can be used to bias any valuation relative to the software technology. Many valuation variables are associated with software source code, such as the number of lines of new and modified code (excluding comments) that were found to be useful in developing reasonableness equations for projected cost of the source code components. The ACM digital library highlighted the reasonableness concern:

> "A basic concern when considering any valuation, or cost to develop, is its reasonableness. A statistical examination should be conducted, to develop a central cost and an acceptable range of values for a software product cost to develop an estimate. The cost estimating of software projects evolved from the works of Walverton attempting to correlate the size of effort in person-months with the size of the product expressed in Thousand Lines of Source Code (KLOC). Large dispersion of data forced others to consider

---

[47] Open source products include permission to use the source code, design documents, or content of the product. It most commonly refers to the open-source model, in which open-source software or other products are released under an open-source license as part of the open-source-software movement.

[48] When you have a math problem that you are working on, and you have worked out the problem and think you have found the solution, a good way to help you make sure is to use reasonableness. In math terms, reasonableness means to verify the answer you have found by either estimating or plugging in your answer to check to see if it works.

additional variables such as programmer experience and the complexity of the application."[49]

In cost modeling, Chris Kemerer[50] suggests that:

"a distinct disadvantage of any formal model is the inconsistency of estimates. He conducted a study indicating that estimates varied from as much as 85% - 610% between predicated and actual values to complete the project[51]. For costing analysis, he suggested calibration of the chosen model can improve these figures, however, formal models still produce errors of 50-100%."

He goes on to say that

"one of the most important objectives of the software engineering community has been the development of useful models that constructively explain the development life-cycle and more accurately predict the cost of developing a software product. To that end, many software estimations models have evolved in the last decades based on the pioneering efforts of the above-mentioned researchers."

Such developments have added greatly to the potential use of such models to predict more accurately fair market values. Especially in those cases when the software product has not achieved market penetration.

In cases of early stage software development (prior to the diffusion

---

[49] ICSE '84 Proceedings of the 7th international conference on Software engineering. From ACM Digital Library

[50] Value your App Inventory, Chris F. Kemerer, InformationWeek of May 25, 1998

[51] Reliability of Function Points Measurement: A Field Experiment; *Comm. ACM,* Vol. 36, *No. 2,* February 1993, pp. 85-97.

stage), we know the value of anything is what someone will pay for it. However, what can we learn from companies who are "in" the software business? How might they approach acquisition of third (3rd) party software inventory items that they intend to include, sell, use or license to others? The "in" companies know that there are many elements to take into consideration, such as;

- has the licensor/seller-maintained IP ownership of the software?
- how did the owner license it (exclusive, field of use limitation, non-exclusive, single use, unlimited corporate), and?
- how many other companies will the owner likely want to license it to, considering the opportunity in the market and its lifecycle?

These are just some concerns the 'in" company will want to resolve. Many "in" companies use a cost model to determine replacement value as a starting price for an acquisition of software that is to be purchased or licensed.

In Purchase Price Allocation[52], when intangible assets are acquired in the purchase of a trade or business, the purchase price must be allocated to the underlying assets and for Federal tax purposes for determining depreciation and amortization allowance under Internal Revenue Codes IRC §167 and §197. The actual allocation is governed by IRC §1060(a) and Reg. §1.1060-1, which require a buyer and seller of a business to allocate the purchase price

---

[52] Purchase Price Allocation (PPA) is an application of goodwill accounting whereby one company (the acquirer), when purchasing a second company (the target), allocates the purchase price into various assets and liabilities acquired from the transaction.

according to the rules of IRC §338(b) (5) and Reg. §338-6. Under this method, the buyer and the seller must use the residual method to allocate the purchase price. It is important to stay on top of all current regulations.

For example, purchase price allocation for financial accounting purposes has in the past undergone significant and complex changes. Accounting Principles Board (APB) Opinion 16 and APB 17 have been superseded by FASB No. 141, Accounting for Business Combinations, and FASB 142, Accounting for Goodwill and Other Intangibles. Under FASB 141 all business combinations must be accounted for using the purchase method, based on the values of the software exchanged. Under FASB 142, goodwill and indefinite-lived intangibles were no longer amortized. Additionally, goodwill and software must be tested annually for asset impairment at the reporting unit level and on an interim basis if an adverse triggering event takes place. As of 2010, corporations that are were planning a business merger had to consider the effect of the transaction under the new rules and plan to carry out a thorough purchase price allocation accordingly. In addition, International Accounting Standards (IASB) had been issued that parallel FASB for financial reporting, consequently, there is a need for experience and expertise to accurately navigate the myriad of valuation issues encountered in a complex software purchase price allocation. There is a need for professionalism and corporate financial governance at its cornerstone.

Properly managing software assets as required in Sarbanes-Oxley[53] (SOX) had never been more important to a corporation's well-

---

[53] The Sarbanes-Oxley Act of 2002 is a law the U.S. Congress passed on July 30 of that year to help protect investors from fraudulent financial reporting by corporations.

being. Granted, the dangers of patent infringement, license violations and counterfeiting have always been a threat to a software owner's profit margin as well as taking media headlines. With regulators' potentially increasing emphasis on transparency and reporting of all material risks to shareholder value, the ability to appraise and keep track of software can mean the difference between weathering a conflict with regulators and having regulatory investigations with a shareholder class action suit piled onto it.

Software inventory assets could account for as much as 80 percent of a company's total market value. Threats to software assets therefore create a very real concern for shareholders. As a result of Sarbanes-Oxley, software financial governance, as of 2010, made it the corporate executives' responsibility, categorizing the company's software asset portfolio, assess the value of each and monitor its use by the company as well as its licensees and even its competitors. Executives are also obligated to foster a culture of compliance and are subject to criminal and civil penalties under the Economic Espionage Act of 1996 for allowing for the misappropriation of third-party trade secrets. Failure to abide by these regulations also could result in inaccurate financial statements which can in turn cause very serious problems for the company.

Responsibility for a company's software intellectual property assets as well as the wellbeing of the remaining inventory assets, had generally fell under the umbrella of the legal department. Unfortunately, in the past, many companies had assigned this task to a person or small department, ill-equipped for this task, not adequately recognizing the potential consequences. By understaffing or improperly controlling a company's software asset inventory portfolio, organizations can both cut into their profit margin and put the company in jeopardy of a shareholder dispute or regulatory inquiry.

Software inventory assets as value is best understood within the framework leading to acceptance of FASB 86, where technology feasibility, management commitment, financial feasibility, ownership statements, and intellectual property rights (such as treating source code as trade secrets), are quality factors, leading to software as a commercial product. Proper management, verification[54], ownership evaluation[55], and valuation[56] provides for governance of software that can be used in establishing and maintaining asset value. Thus, identification (with both verification and ownership evaluation) of the components, and controlled access to the components, makes value and future use possible.

For example, as stated in FASB 141/142 a component value for a software asset must be established in a Merger or Acquisition. The allocation of that value must be done with consideration to future potential. Even in an acquisition by license of a software product, access by the licensee, to the software source code and other inventory components of that software product may be mandatory and critical in the ability to maintain the value of that software acquisition, especially if the license is for a critical software product and the licensor goes out of business (more on risks later).

The website article in webopedia.com on ownership of software,

---

[54] the process of establishing the truth, accuracy, or validity of something

[55] the making of a judgment about the validity or assessment of ownership

[56] an estimation of something's worth, especially one carried out by a professional appraiser

"What happens when you purchase a specific software application? And if you've purchased software, what is the license agreement for? Do you now own the software because you paid for it? Simply put, no. Though you may have paid for the software, what you have done is licensed the application, essentially paying for the rights to use the software according to guidelines determined by the owner. The owner of the software remains the person or entity that holds the sole legal authority power to sell, distribute, copy and/or change the content of the software. And unless the person or organization transfers ownership rights, the rights remain with the owner no matter how many times the owner legally distributes the software. When a user either purchases software or freely downloads software from the internet, the user is not buying the ownership rights to the software but a license to use the software according to the licensing agreement, or EULA (for end user licensing agreement). The EULA is a legal agreement between the two parties and is legally actionable if either party violates the terms of the agreement. *It should be noted that the software referred to herein is proprietary software, not open source software, which follows its own set of rules."[57]

However, in an acquisition by purchase of a software company, or in an investment requiring software as collateral, access to all the software inventory components of that software product are mandatory and critical in the ability to maintain the value of that acquisition or investment. Thus, investments with proper risk management, evaluation, and analysis of the components with

---

[57] See webopedia.com/DidYouKnow/Hardware_Software/OwningSoftware.asp

their total valuation and verification can help provide for governance that can be used in establishing and maintaining asset value and making money.

Chapter 3

Software valuation methods

Regulations may govern the method for determining an appropriate value of an item or software product in a specific context. But they often admit the possibility of using other, unspecified, methods. For example, the selection of the appropriate transfer pricing valuation method relies on the "best method" rule; Comparable Uncontrolled Transaction Method (CUT), Comparable Profit Margin Method (CPM), or Profit-Split Methods (PSM) and all three admits the use of unspecified methods, such as replacement cost analysis. But whichever method is selected for the purpose, all methods determine a value which should be commensurate with the software product and its future ability for monetizing (licensing and other service revenue).

Determining the values of all the components of a software product inventory can be most problematic. As mentioned earlier, non-software patent and trademark components have a long history of many valuation contexts, but not necessarily the 'software patent'[58]. Thus, for the software patent, valuation may be

---

[58] Neither software nor computer programs are explicitly mentioned in statutory United States patent law. Patent law has changed to address new technologies, and decisions of the United States Supreme Court and United States Court of Appeals for the Federal Circuit (CAFC) beginning in the latter part of the 20th century have sought to clarify the boundary between patent-eligible and patent-ineligible subject matter for a number of new technologies including computers and software. The first computer software case in the Supreme Court was *Gottschalk v. Benson* in 1972. Since then, the Supreme Court has decided about a half dozen cases touching on the patent eligibility of software-related inventions. The eligibility of software, as such, for patent protection has been only scantily addressed in the court or in legislation. In fact, in the recent Supreme Court decision in *Alice v. CLS Bank*, the Court painstakingly avoided the issue, and one Justice in the oral argument repeatedly insisted that it was unnecessary to reach the issue. The expression "software patent" itself has not been clearly defined. The United States Patent and Trademark Office (USPTO) has permitted patents to be issued on nothing more than a series of software computer instructions, but the latest Federal Circuit decision on the subject invalidated such a patent. The court held that software instructions as such were too intangible to fit within any of the statutory categories such as machines or articles of manufacture. On June 19, 2014 the United States Supreme Court ruled in *Alice Corp. v. CLS Bank International* that "merely requiring generic computer implementation

problematic. Even for the other software inventory components, valuation methods are not as developed as valuation methods for tangibles.

To compound this issue, many valuation experts disagree even on which method is best for valuing different types of software, for example operating system software vs website software. Current valuation methods for fair value of any the software components generally fall within one of the three categories:

- the Cost Approach for valuing software based on how much it costs to create or recreate that asset,
- the Income (Net Present Value) approach for valuing software products based on all revenue (licensing, support, and maintenance), and
- the Market approach for valuing software based on the licensing, patent royalty rates (if included in the software product), or sales of similar software products from one company to another.

Experts say that while you may use any one of the three approaches to reliably estimate value, it is best to compare the results obtained by using two approaches to sufficiently challenge the results and determine a likely range of value for a software transaction context. So, is there a best software valuation approach for all components? As mentioned earlier, the best method of valuation is based on an appropriate context be it for tax, management, merger, acquisition, collateral surety, and etc.

The various methods employed by professionals who analyze

---

fails to transform [an] abstract idea into a patent-eligible invention. See wikipedia.org/wiki/Software_patents...

intellectual asset for market and fair values are cost, market, and income methods. These three methods are also the basics in valuing intellectual property assets and the experts recommend multiple valuations to reach a final determination of market or fair value. According to the experts, each of these methods of valuation has limitations, but together they can provide a set of very useful decision-making tools. Thus, for software use licensing (assuming nonexclusive) the cost replacement methods valuation might lend credibility to a specific royalty or license fee discussion with the licensee. If one is looking at an M&A opportunity or investment opportunity into a company, the income method will most likely be used by the acquiring or investing organization and it is best if the potential acquired software company understands that. A savvy software company should know the market value of its software product using a Net Present Value (NPV) calculation. However, the software company may want to attempt to get a valuation price higher based upon increasing the value by using the other component asset factors for positive adjustments. The most common adjustment is done by discussing the patent portfolio and how it could protect a market position. A more complete discussion of the valuation might be using the other inventory component valuations to provide unique positioning and future multiple product income streams.

The income method may be appropriate in licensing situations where there may be exclusivity in the license. Even if the use of the income method in early stage software development of a new software product is problematic, most financial folks will want to do an income projection even with a very questionable forecasting. But, when you are looking at early stage software (prior to the diffusion stage), the income streams may be inappropriate no matter how well you think someone can forecast.

An issue in pre-FASB No. 86 was commercial applicability for a computer software product. The released FASB statement identified the costs to be expensed, costs to be capitalized, and it specified amortization, disclosure, and other requirements. But, from the corporate governance perspective are not all costs involved in developing all components of a software product inventory, required to bring a software product to full monetization, the real 'ownership' value of the software product?

For the ownership value of a software product's total inventory, one needs to deal with the sum (or bundle) of the component values that will make a software product commercial or useful. A formula to establish an ownership value, using pre-FASB No. 86 influencing factors as a base, was developed by Data Securities International[59] (DSI). DSI was a software proprietary deposit and software source code escrow[60] company, that also provided verification and validation to the escrow requested by many companies for the purposes of;

- establishing management values for shareholder equity, debt financing, merger and acquisitions, and
- a fair market value for a software product prior to market launch.

The basic formula developed by Data Securities International for

---

[59] Acquired by Iron Mountain in 1997 see wiki data securities international

[60] Source code escrow is the deposit of the source code of software with a third-party escrow agent. Escrow is typically requested by a party licensing software (the licensee), to ensure maintenance of the software instead of abandonment or orphaning. The software's source code is released to the licensee if the licensor files for bankruptcy or otherwise fails to maintain and update the software as promised in the software license agreement. See Wikipedia source code escrow.

software management was Total Software Value (TSV) equals the sum of:

- Ownership Value (OV) multiplied by the Composite of Influencing Factors (CIF) plus
- Market Value (MV) plus
- Internal Cost Savings (ISC).

That is TSV = (OV*CIF) + MV + ISC. This formula provided for software developed for commercial use to be valued for a variety of management purposes. Potentially each valuation could be used independently or as a summation. As you would expect, the quality influencing factors (CIF) were technology feasibility, management commitment, financial feasibility, and ownership of intellectual property rights. If these factors were less than one (1), they would weigh heavily on a company's ownership valuation. If TSV-OV was zero (0), then there was basically no ownership value. There are other factors that apply in software valuations and will be discussed in later chapters.

For software product companies the TSV valuation made sense. The pre-FASB No. 86 rule did not specifically call out intellectual property rights as a requirement, but, if you don't have the work for hire agreement and copyright assignment statements for the software product components, then, you really don't own the intellectual property. If you are missing the ownership value, TSV-OV = 0, what can you do with the software to extract revenue opportunity. Corporate governance of software needs to consider all the quality factors discussed prior to the release of FASB No. 86. The TSV and influencing factors can be used by any company that needs to manage the software they purchased or plan to license to the marketplace.

In my experience, see authors bio Exhibit, software product companies prior to 2015, had done little to assign TSV-OV governance values. For sure, market value, TSV-MV, but ownership value for management oversight seemed to be missing. Applying management responsibility based upon value principles seemed to be missing. Maybe SOX and FAS 141/142 and future new governance requirements will require changes. The idea that management is judged based upon whether the software asset TSV value is increased or decreased under management decisions might still be missing at the governance level. In my opinion, reasonable software product governance has its base in the TSV-OV ownership value of the asset inventory.

The software product inventory is considered to include both intellectual property (IP) and intellectual assets (IA). Like Vertex of Canada, "one could consider traditional IP to comprise just the patents, trade-marks, copyrights and industrial design registrations, because these four intellectual properties have legislation to protect the legal owners in the disclosure (license) of these assets".[61] Non disclosed intellectual assets (IA) in the software inventory would then be trade secrets, unpublished copyrights, know-how, source code, data bases, and the codified tangible descriptions of specific knowledge which a business uses to support commercialization. Trade secrets, unpublished copyrights, and know-how are those software inventory assets that contain valuable proprietary information that belongs exclusively to the business, and which is used in the business to provide economic or competitive advantage. Many proprietary software

---

[61] Intellectual Asset Identification, The First Step in an Intellectual Property Management Program, Dave Tyrrell and Gary Floyd, Vertex Intellectual Property Strategies Inc.

vendors consider trade secrets to include unpatented inventions, formulas, processes, devices, patterns, designs, design drawings, source code, customer databases, and internal operations manuals. Fundamentally, these software business companies do the due diligence of defining how their software fits as part of their overall corporate strategy. Others may consider software to be just an end because any value to the company is very hard to quantify.

Due diligence done by software companies develop answers to SWOT analysis questions;
- Is this software core to the value I bring to my clients?
- Is this software non-core?
- Does this software inventory component provide a competitive advantage?
- Can I maximize re-use across other platforms?
- Can I re-use software inventory components across other software products?
- What does the SWOT (Strengths, Weakness, Opportunities, Threats) matrix look like?

Chapter 4

Software governance and Total Software Value (TSV)

The intangible assets owned by a software enterprise, include: the technical knowledge, know-how of its staff, the competence of its sales force, the business experience knowledge of its management, its goodwill and reputation, trademarks, the value of its intellectual property, the commercial value of its licenses, and the value of its software inventory.

There is a need to accurately identify, analyze, and evaluate intangible assets within an enterprise as regulations force governance of these assets. Some questions asked;
- which software inventory assets have market value?

- which software inventory assets can be monetized? and
- what are the values, whether as a capital asset or as a debt security?

A very significant amount of time has passed since the American Institute of Certified Public Accountants (AICPA) Statement of Position 98-1 (SOP 98-1)[62] and the Financial Accounting Standards Board (FASB) Statement No. 86 was approved. According to many experts, however, both standards exhibit a weakness in software attributes, and particularly as it relates to what financial information is important to provide.

FASB's Statement No. 86 and AICPA's Statement of Position 98-1 are accounting concerning on how software assets should appear on corporate financial statements. However, some current proposals on software valuation, such as by 'Mordechai Ben-Menachem and Ilanit Gavious'[63] believe that the techniques, models and concepts used by these standards have not kept pace with software advancements, such as those commonly used in costing and development life cycle models for creating and maintaining software assets.

> "The past accounting treatment of software was as if it were a mechanical device, such as the case under FASB No. 86, resulted in a misunderstanding and potentially incorrect valuation of software. The fact is that only a small fraction of the costs associated with the development of software is

---

[62] AICPA Statement of Position No. 98-1 specifies that the capitalization of costs begins when 1. The preliminary stage is completed, 2. management authorizes and commits to funding a company software project, and 3. interest costs are incurred when developing the software.

[63] Accounting Software Assets: A Valuation Model for Software, Journal of Information Systems, Fall *2007*

traditionally recognized as an asset, while most of those costs are immediately expensed as they are incurred. Consequently, the true value of software is immensely underestimated on the balance sheet."[64]

To compound such undervaluation, 'Hughes and Cotterell in their Business Performance Management'[65] article, discussed FASB's Statement No. 86 and AICPA's Statement of Position (SOP) 98-1, where capitalizable costs are principally restricted to certain development costs that do not include the costs of the software's future modification, improvement, and general evolution. They imply that this

> "may produce an un-intended effect in the current accounting treatment of software that leads to a disproportionate downward bias in the reported fair value of software. Indeed, costs incurred for such on-going software evolution may be five (5) to twenty (20) times the original development costs that are incurred for the software's first release."[66]

In addition to undervaluation problems resulting from only capitalizing a small part of software's costs, both accounting standards are based on an outmoded system lifecycle model that is essentially incorrect. FASB's Statement No. 86 and AICPA's Statement of Position 98-1 both use the same basic model.[67] This

---

[64] ibid

[65] Business Performance Management (BPM) Forum, 2004 article

[66] ibid

[67] Accounting Software Assets: A Valuation Model for Software, Journal of Information Systems, Fall 2007

model is very similar to the waterfall model[68] first described by Winston Royce[69] in 1970, ironically as an example of a flawed model for software development. The software engineering community has not used this method because it leads to misleading and untrustworthy project results. In fact, software products (internal or external) are almost always put into use with only partial functional requirements fulfilled, and then evolve over time (frequently, over very long times) as the software is enhanced, customized, adapted and new requirements are discovered and changed.[70] One of the greatest inherent value of software is its ability evolve and adapt to new business challenges through modifications, revisions and continuous improvement.

Another valuation problem arises when overhead development costs are not to be capitalized even if management believes such overhead is incremental to the software project.

"The current accounting standards only allows a company to capitalize costs that are directly associated with developing or obtaining the software, such as materials, services and payroll-related cost for specific employees. Therefore, it has been proposed that not only is software immensely undervalued in the balance sheet, but current

---

[68] the waterfall model is a software development process. The waterfall model emphasizes that a logical progression of steps be taken throughout the software development life cycle (SDLC), much like the cascading steps down an incremental waterfall.

[69] Winston Walker Royce (August 15, 1929 – June 7, 1995) was an American computer scientist, director at Lockheed Software Technology Center in Austin, Texas. He was a pioneer in the field of software development, known for his 1970 paper from which the Waterfall model for software development was mistakenly drawn.

[70] Accounting Software Assets: A Valuation Model for Software, Journal of Information Systems, Fall 2007

earnings are also excessively depressed by immediate expensing of most software costs. As a result, in an era where most business activities essentially rely on information technology (IT) systems, reported earnings become less reliable and less relevant for investment decisions."[71]

The capitalization standard for software development was often and aggressively criticized. Years ago, the software Publishers Association (SPA) wrote a letter to FASB stating

"We do not believe software development costs are a useful predictive factor of future product sales and the users of financial statements have a high degree of skepticism when it comes to soft assets resulting from the capitalization of software development costs."[72]

Of course, respondents to the SPA counter claimed that the current method of software capitalization is relevant to investors. Yet, analysis made by Kevin Den-Adel[73] implied that a full capitalization of software development costs with uniform amortization is more value relevant than the current accounting practice, which may explain a reason for the variation in stock prices.[74]

---

[71] ibid

[72] Software Publishers Association, letter to FASB dated March 14, 1996

[73] Kevin Den Adel, an accounting lecturer and the Director of the Undergraduate Accounting Program at the University of Iowa, encourages business owners to reconsider their accounting strategies. He believes that an improved accounting department can pinpoint areas of a business that need to be adjusted in order to achieve a maximum profit margin

[74] The Value Reference of Alternative Accounting Treatments of Software Development Costs, University of Iowa - Department of Accounting, September 10, 1999

Generally Accepted Accounting Principles[75] (GAAP) tend to treat 'purchased' and 'developed' assets differently with purchased recorded as an asset at purchase price, regardless of how the asset was originally produced. In the case of developed software, SOP 98-1 required a differentiation between costs that are expensed and those that can be recorded as assets. The discernment of what is an asset via where the costs occurred is not relevant to asset-value. The proper discernment must be between cost of creative processes that create objects (components) and non-creative processes that manipulate existing objects.[76] SOP 98-1 did not recognize objects, only some of the input occurrences material to the formation of some objects. This does not match the concept of asset as object. The conclusion is that accounting must recognize that software is an object.[77]

In the Mythical Man Month Essays,

> "Whereas computer hardware may deteriorate from normal 'wear and tear' over the course of its ordinary use, software is strengthened and enhanced by use, and only loses value as a result of inherent defects that remain uncorrected or where the business premise for its original functionality changes and renders the fundamental operation of the software obsolete"[78].

---

[75] Generally accepted accounting principles, or GAAP, are a set of rules that encompass the details, complexities, and legalities of business and corporate accounting. The Financial Accounting Standards Board (FASB) uses GAAP as the foundation for its comprehensive set of approved accounting methods and practices
[76] Accounting Software Assets: A Valuation Model for Software, Journal of Information Systems, Fall *2007*
[77] Ibid
[78] The Mythical Man Month: Essays on Software Engineering, Addison-Wesley, 1995

Software product valuations could be better understood by looking at the processes through which a software product is created and evolved than by looking at the mere cost of labor associated with its original partial development. Focusing on only direct, hard programmer costs (for example payroll), while ignoring the overall investment in the processes, project, and other development outputs, misunderstands the true investment that is required for software commercialization, which leads to non-governance and under valuation of such software. Today, software products are built by software researchers, designers, programmers, engineers, quality assurance, document writers, system and market analysts, etc., all with highly integrated, multi-disciplinary knowledgebases that provide added value to the software inventory.

If one values software on a governance and fair value basis than one must consider not only direct, first-release, project costs, but also all the developments and processes that burn through most of the money. If so then it may be possible to provide meaningful information for financial management of software as well as dealing intelligently with software revenue recognition. However, without understanding all the issues, we had many numerous confusions on value vs. revenue that are still being untangled.

Software products are rarely licensed on a stand-alone basis. More often, they are licensed as a package including; upgrades, maintenance, special services, training, customer specific enhancements, hardware interfaces, and installation services. A software license is typically negotiated as a whole, with the license forming the basis for the relationship. This inevitably raises two financial issues; first, how to allocate revenue among the components, and then how to allocate revenue among accounting periods if components and services are delivered over more than one reporting period.

Under United States (US) GAAP, no software revenue can be recognized unless a signed license agreement exists. US GAAP rules stated that where customary practice is to obtain a signed contract (license), no revenue may be recognized until a final written contract has been signed by both parties. Thus, no revenue may be recognized until the license is signed even if fees have been paid and certain components and services delivered.

Under SOP 97-2[79], the total license revenue must be allocated among the components of a license in proportion to the revenue value of each component, regardless of the prices specified in the contract. However, revenue may only be recognized if there is Vendor-Specific Objective Evidence (VSOE) of revenue value for each component in the license, or when the revenue value of all undelivered components is known. SOP 97-2 stipulated that VSOE can only exist if the component in question is also sold separately. Rarely in software product licensing are software upgrades, maintenance, special services, training, customer specific enhancements, hardware interfaces, and installation services always offered separately. Thus, if there is no VSOE of revenue value, no revenue can be recognized, although there was exception for software maintenance.

This concept implied that revenue value could not be measured using estimated costs for completion of the components or services

---

[79] According to SOP 97-2 software revenue recognition, the price must be fair value as established by the market. To show proof of VSOE, firms needed to collect sales transactions for each separate element of a contract and determine the average price for these transactions

to be delivered. The only factor that could be considered in practice is the price of the component when licensed separately. Applying this rule had created numerous problems for companies in practice. For example: If the element is never licensed separately, there can be no VSOE of value. Licenses often include rights to future versions, products or enhancements, which, by definition, are not yet available. Consequently, there can be no VSOE of fair value for these elements. A software company therefore could not potentially recognize any revenue on delivered elements (components) so long as there are undelivered elements for which no VSOE of fair value exists.[80]

In management valuation, one must first recognize that software is a valuable business asset. Identification of software assets needs to focus on software products and components that are developed by a business for commercialization. In that context, most software products could be categorized as follows:
- software product (developed for internal use or external licensing),
- embedded software (typically in special hardware such as in equipment or in a cell phone),
- databases managed by software, and
- website software (content, service, etc.) in the software product category.

In considering the Federal issues discussed, one might question whether a non-specialized accountant or auditor was qualified to provide accurate, up-to-date and reliable information concerning

---

[80] Price Waterhouse Coopers - A shifting software revenue recognition landscape? Insights on potential impacts of IFRS and US GAAP convergence.
www.pwc.com/extweb/pwcpublications.nsf/docid/568C611407DEAAE4852573E200 06A7D5/$FILE/shiftingsoftware.pdf

software governance or fair value calculations. Could any accounting audit have provided enough information for governance undertaking where the software inventory, as a significant and expensive group of assets are essentially absent from corporate management's or an investor's view? The hidden business value of such software assets could have had potentially significant implications. While in the past the inability to account for software value means that its contributions to an enterprise's true value are not reflected on the enterprise's income statement or balance sheet, the lack of an accurate valuation may have also hampered any stakeholders' decision-making ability.

We should consider a more reliable valuation model for software based upon measurements of software that take into full account all the costs incurred to create the software inventory and their feasibility factors. In this model, costs can be collected by an automatic tool and stored in a database of software enterprise assets and costs added to the effect of each individual module's relative significance to the enterprise.[81] This cost model provided a systematic algorithm for software amortization, based on the decrease in its usability (or commercial value). TSV software analysis therefore recognized that the intrinsic value of a software product must include all costs incurred in the software's development. That calculation will include the costs incurred prior to capitalization, as well as costs incurred after first release. These measurements could ideally be collected in a software inventory system.[82]

---

[81] Accounting Software Assets: A Valuation Model for Software, Journal of Information Systems, Fall 2007
[82] ibid

Any software product inventory system should be designed to provide accurate and up-to-date information concerning software's product components and recognition of all related evaluation of the software components. Such a scheme should show all software component assets hierarchically with their relationship, history, complexity, other influencing factors, and costs incurred. This information could also be useful in other valuation models for computing context driven valuations for software and appropriate software-based IP protections. This system could provide for information necessary for setting software risk and influencing factors that can be applied to valuation calculations. Hopefully, this could lead to better governance, monetization and valuation of software products.

A Total Software Value (TSV) uses the software inventory composites of ownership value (OV), market value (MV), and internal cost savings (ICS) as values and influencing factor variables of software as a management asset tool.[83] Of course the potential market value could be a staggering, but it is in the governance of the inventory that assures the market value. A TSV software inventory valuation (OV) analysis (see Exhibit G)[84] looked at the total of the bundles of the various software components or intellectual assets that make software usable as a product. The following three tables and Exhibit help highlight these software product asset inventory components for analysis and governance.

Table 1 is a view of the various bundle types of Intellectual assets and intellectual property involved and a list of some of the typical components in each bundle. The items listed on the left side of

[83] Software & Valuation in the Information Society, LES Nouvelles, June 2008
[84] TSV information request about a software inventory, developed by the author

Table 1 are typically known or available to the market. The items on the right are the background assets owned by the software owner and are what professor Karl Jorda hints to in his comment "Patents are but the tips of icebergs in a sea of trade secrets.... patents have value and possibly more valuable are the background assets."[85]

Table 1: Software IP Bundles	
1. Marketing and Sales	2. Trade Secrets and Know How
• Marketing plans and collateral	• Design documentation
3. Patent(s)	• Source code
• Defensive and offensive	• Formulas
4. Copyrights	• Process know how
• Executable code	• Operating platforms
• User documentation	• Manufacturing instructions
• Installation instructions	• Configuration data
• GUI's	• QA test and procedures
5. Domain Name(s)	• 3rd party software
6. Licenses	• SAAS or ASP databases
• Encumbrances	• Client databases

---

[85] The Differences between Patent and Trade Secret, Franklin Pierce Law School, Summer/Fall 2004

Table 2 attempts to highlight the right side of Table 1's 'Trade Secret and know how' background components that are typically produced during the development cycles for a software product.

Table 2: Software—Intangible Asset Inventory	
1. Marketing and Sales	2. License Management
• Marketing plans and collateral	• DRM and license controls
3. Client Support Systems	• Back office system
• Installation and training	4. R&D Systems
• User documentation and help	• Internal Design Documentation
• Client databases	• Source code with comments
5. QA and Testing	• Source code control with comments
• Bug/support system	• ASP databases
• Testing code and data	• QA test and procedures
6. Manufacturing System	• 3rd party software
• Specific build guides	• Open source & strategy
7. Commercialization Strategy	• Client databases
• Product plan (release and updates)	

Table 3 highlights the complexity at stake in determining which Federal disclosure protection may be used with each software component (bundle) as each of the identified components can be protected by different types of intellectual property rights.

Software Component	Copyright	Trademarks	Patents	Trade Secrets
Table 3: Software Components as Intellectual Property				
GUIs	√	√		√
Source code	√	√	√	√
Object code	√			
Business processes	√	√	√	√
Data	√	√		√
Table structures	√			√
Documentation internal design and external use	√	√		√

Chapter 5

The software inventories

It is during the innovation and syndication stage of software development where software intellectual property begin to take shape and software patent, trademark, and copyright emerge and sometimes collide (see Table 3). In these early stages there is often confusion as to if a software patent should be applied for and even if a software patent is appropriate for protection. Does a software patent really have value apart from protection of the software product released and the inventory components?

Can one really value a software patent, outside the context of the software inventory? If there is no intent to commercialize then there is possibly no software inventory. If there is no software inventory, then any valuation apart from the patent portfolio becomes problematic (see past chapter). Software patent only monetization is outside the scope of this book.

> *Editor Notes: In patent only licensing with no reduction to practice, and only the claims exist, is outside the scope of this book. It is important to realize that some patents come into existence for market monopoly, design, and for portfolio management purposes that can be used in cross licensing and are outside the discussion of this book.*
>
> *I provide a link to the great work done by Dr. Paul Germeraad to pull together some great articles on technology and patent portfolio management.*
> *See www.businessinnovationmanagement.com*

Aura Soininen[86] stated in her thesis regarding the value of patents without reduction to practice.

> "The value of a patent is dependent on the value of the invention it claims, and how it is commercialized. Thus, most of them are worth very little, and most inventions are not worth patenting: it may be possible to protect them in

---

[86] Aura Soininen, who has worked in the IP and technology group of B&K's Helsinki office since 2005, has completed her dissertation on patents. The public examination of the work titled "Patents in the Information and Communications Technology Sector - Development Trends, Problem Areas and Pressures for Change" was held on 3 March 2007 in the Lappeenranta University of Technology.

other ways, and the costs of protection may exceed the benefits."[87]

In the innovation and syndication stages of any software product, the manpower projects involved produce a quantity of inventory components. If a component was needed that is why the component came into existence. Someone determined that the component was needed to achieve a return on investment for the software product or service. The critical issue is whether those component assets are development errors and are of no interest in governance and valuation or are they in fact assets in the sense that, for management decisions, stakeholders need to receive information concerning their use and value? These components need to be identified and governed, just as all other "hard" assets. No one would ever think of "not managing" the physical inventory in buildings, or machines, yet historically for software, a black hole seemed to be the norm. Software governance must be on the total inventory and be managed to be of value. It is not rocket science to guess that inventory components that have not been valued seem to go unnoticed. The basic requirement for governance is an accurate and up-to-date inventory of all software components, showing any hierarchy (updates) with history, complexity and all costs incurred.

Changes to software components are constant and these changes must be reflected in the software inventory database. There is no technological reason to not differentiate valuations of "initial development" and valuations that occur later. Valuations change as

---

[87] Patents in the Information and Communications Technology Sector - Development Trends, Problem Areas and Pressures for Change, Aura Soininen, ISBN 978-952-214-344-0 (PDF) 2007

the component changes and are usually associated with events that occurred after the initial release of the software product. In many instances additional costs incurred increase the value of the component. Also, for governance each component will need to have associated risk and influencing factors that affect its valuation.

To the basic components in the software inventory, risk and influencing factors should be factored in. But what risk and influencing factors? In software development, software risk and influencing factors are called Control by Importance and Exception (CIE) factors.[88] In this Ben-Gurion University paper there is a discussion of a technological-view mapping between actual costs and an individual module's importance to the enterprise (remembering that all software is multi-level, hierarchical and granular). The view of a module's technological importance provides accounting with a valid basis for estimating sensitivity and, hence, a risk factor, accounted for in the software valuation.[89] In this paper, sensitivity refers to the "degree of care" needed when making a change in a module. In this article five quantifiable parameters control sensitivity:

- reuse count,
- application mission criticality,
- complexity,
- updating difficulty, and
- internal functionality or interface implementation.[90]

The Reuse factor from the article,

---

[88] IT Assets: Control by Importance and Exception; a Paradigm of Change Support technology. Working paper 2003, Ben-Gurion University,
[89] ibid
[90] ibid

"Reuse count refers to the quantity of uses for this module. For example, in a bank, a module which computes interest may be used to compute interest for many different types of accounts, though each account type may be implemented via a different system. Additional uses of a module mean the module has been more expensive to produce but this additional use has a payback by reducing expense in other projects utilizing it. A common platform is more difficult and more expensive to produce, but much more cost-effective to the enterprise. However, if a change is made in this platform, those that change it must consider all of its users."[91]

In any software product TSV valuation, the corresponding software inventory should be valued for the current and prior year. Any positive or negative delta variance will provide another risk or influencing factor for biasing the estimated valuation. These valuations may also help management understand and govern any software asset impairment should there be a negative variance.

In pre-FASB No. 86, there are different influencing factors at play that more aptly apply to market value and management governance. One might be cautioned in preparing any valuation to include the CIE factors and CIF influencing factors. Also not present in 1985 during the development of FASB No. 86 was the world of open source's risks and benefits. Today, software valuations should include the risk influencing factor of open source. For example, the mingling of open source code in proprietary software may imposes a significant risk or influencing factor that may reduce or even increase the total software value. The two most significant issues are that of ownership and patent portfolio management.

---

[91] ibid

Chapter 6

Ownership value of software

As mentioned, Data Securities International introduced a software valuation concept, Total Software Value (TSV) in the late 1980's. This valuation concept uses the ownership value (TSV-OV) (of the software inventory), market value (TSV-MV), and internal cost savings (TSV-ICS) as values with influencing variables when considering software as a management asset for governance. It is important to state that TSV is not an investing, tax, or accounting fair value[92].

---

[92] In investing, fair value refers to an asset's sale price agreed upon by a willing buyer and seller. In accounting, fair value represents the estimated worth of various assets and liabilities that must be listed on a company's financial statement.

A software inventory valuation or TSV-OV analysis looks at the sum total of all the various software inventory components that make a software product. The TSV-OV sum value is then biased by composite of influencing factor (CIF) factors, to more closely project a management value for the product's software inventory. As discussed earlier, each software inventory asset value should be biased and managed by the influencing (CIF) and exception (CIE) factors. For a software market fair valuation, one might use a discounted cash flow method to compute an interim market value for the parties to consider. A software valuation for internal cost savings or TSV-ICS analysis looks at the software within the enterprise to determine an anticipated license value and subsequent cost savings. This chapter takes a closer look at the TSV-OV valuation process and subsequent chapters will discuss on TSV-MV and TSV-ICS valuations.

The software inventory is also made up of know-how, trade secrets, and unpublished copyrights that are often used to describe some or all the same software components. It is during the innovation and syndication stages of development when the software inventory for a software product comes into existence. There is often confusion as to what software assets to include in a software product valuation or how to value each type of software asset. For example, at the first launch of a software product into the market, can one really believe any forecasted number of licenses or services to compute a market value based on forecasted future sales?

How does a newly registered trademark really have asset value for a non-established software product? And, for a software patent, is there really any blocking monopoly value yet? Why would one want a monopoly if a market is not yet established? In many new product cases, one would want as many competitors in the field as possible to help establish the market? It is also important to remember that for a new software product, it is only after the market has been established and demand is apparent that there is real market value. Before that, the background software inventory components are the only assets with some ownership value.

Thankfully, software patent protection does not require the disclosure of all related software product components necessary for market acceptance and penetration, but only that which is required to cover the claims. For proprietary software the open disclosure of any components may decrease the proprietary software products market potential and may increase immediate competition.

However, in the open source community, disclosure of certain source code may increase market penetration and acceptance. In either case, trade secrets, know how, and other background components that may not be disclosed (except for the software components downloaded, such as in SourceForge[93]) are considered proprietary and for internal use only by their owner.

In a TSV-OV valuation all the software inventory components need to be identified, evaluated and valued. The table below lists some of the various components that are typically produced during the development of a software product. One of the software asset components, called the "source codes", are typically the costliest to produce, test, and document, and in most cases, arguably the

---

[93] SourceForge is a web-based service that offers software developers a centralized online location to control and manage free and open-source software projects the open source forge

most valuable. These components are used to further illustrate a TSV-OV valuation.

Gordon Smith in his IP valuation book suggested that one method to measure fair market value is its cost to replace.[94]

Software – Intangible Asset Inventory

Marketing and Sales	License Management
Marketing documents	DRM and license controls
Client Support Systems	Back office system
Installation and training	R&D Systems
User documentation	Internal Design Documentation
Client databases	Source code with comments
QA and testing	Source code with comments
Bug/support system	ASP databases
Testing code and data	QA test and procedures
Manufacturing System	3rd Party software
Specific build guides	Open Source & Strategy
7. Commercialization	
Product plan	

Typical software valuations have historically examined the financial statements for either the capitalized software costs[95], defined by Financial Accounting Standards Board No. 86, or attempts to break out a portion of R&D expenses that could be allocated to the software. A much more rational approach is to ask experts, such as those that had developed software and are now in the valuation business, to value and evaluate the software inventory. They can

---

[94] Valuation of Intellectual Property and Intangible Assets, Third Edition, Gordon Smith and Russell Parr
[95] Software Valuation in the Information Society, LES Nouvelles, June 2008

predict the cost to develop a component that would be or would have to be paid to have a similar software asset built?

A replacement value can be calculated using software costing models that can be compared to the cost based on actual historical data. For example, a TSV-OV valuation for source code (evaluated without inclusion of comments) is best done using an estimated replacement cost method for determining a reasonable ownership value at the end of the syndication phase. One might also consider the time value factor in using the TSV-OV as the fair market valuation between the two parties.

Unlike most valuations that only value to the first release, a total software valuation (TSV) can be designed to look at all the developments and projects that consume most of the money involved in the development of a software product. Indeed, by using this technique a meaningful ownership valuation can be done at any version release in the diffusion stage of a software product.

One method of valuation for the software inventory is to look at the results of a software project estimation model to determine if its estimate is reasonable for a cost to replace value. According to the experts in software cost modeling, experience suggested that no single technique is best for all development contexts. If we were only using a software cost model to project cost, then a comparison of results of several model approaches is most likely to produce a more realistic cost estimate.

Typically, software engineering cost models and estimation techniques are used for several purposes. These include budgeting, risk analysis, project planning, cost control, and schedule breakdowns by component. This process can be done for software improvement investment analysis. TSV-OV expands the list to include the management value of the software inventory's source codes. In selecting the cost model for TSV-OV it is recommended using one that biases the cost based on historical data. The purpose of such is to determine if the economic value computed by the cost model is reasonable compared to similar efforts.

There are a number of databases that contain information on similar efforts such as COCOMO[96] (COnstructive COst MOdel), as well as other sizing data such as that associated with the verification results which has been gathered by Data Securities International (DSI)[97] over its 20-year history until its acquisition by Iron Mountain.[98]

To complicate the discussion of the inventory valuation of software, one must consider what happens to software value over time during its life cycle in the marketplace. It is here where software differs importantly from computer hardware tangible assets. Successful software products typically have many versions, long lifetimes, and corresponding high maintenance cost ratios over their lifetime. A software product lifetime, before complete product (not version) substitution, was 10 to 15 years and are likely to increase in the future.[99] New version release frequency is determined by the rate of required bug fixes needed and the tolerance of users to dealing with upgrades. Many examples in the past have shown an average rate of 18 months for an update version releases. With well-maintained software, in active use,

---

[96] Software Development Cost Estimation Approaches – A Survey, Barry Boehm, Chris Abts University, Sunita Chulani IBM Research
[97] Now Iron Mountain
[98] Iron Mountain acquired DSI in 1997
[99] What is Your Software Worth? Gio Wiederhold Stanford University April 2007

does not wear out, and is likely to gain value.[100] The majority of software costs are often incurred during the period after the first release to the marketplace and acceptance by industry.

Accordingly, successful enterprise software products have many versions, long lifetimes, and corresponding high maintenance cost ratios over their lifetime. Maintenance costs of such enterprise software amounted to 60% to 90% of its total costs.[101] These costs are primarily due to software maintenance, which refers both to the activities to preserve the software's existing functionality and performance, and activities to increase its functionality and improve its performance throughout the life-cycle.[102] Thus, over that life, there may have been 10 significant version releases. Early in a software products life, there may have been several versions per year. Software that is significantly dependent on external conditions will require more frequent updates.

In "What is Your Software Worth" by Gio Wiederhold, suggested
> "that one should measure code sizes of software versions to allocate its relative contribution. This approach assumed that the value of a unit of the original code is just as valuable as a unit of new code."

Wiederhold suggested there are valid arguments that code size is not a surrogate for the value content of the product. One argument was that later code, being more recent, represents more recent innovation, and hence should be valued higher. However, an argument in the opposite direction is that the basic functionality is

---

[100] Ibid
[101] Thomas M. Pigoski: *Practical Software Maintenance - Best Practices for Managing Your Software Investment*; IEEE Computer Society Press, 1997.
[102] Software Development Cost Estimation Approaches – A Survey, Barry Boehm, Chris Abts University, Sunita Chulani IBM Research

represented by the initial code. There may have been a few lines of brilliant initial code, slowly buried in a mass of subsequent system interfaces and later tweaks and fixes, which are critical to any intellectual asset. Wiederhold goes on to suggest,

> "one might find that much code is inserted later to deal with error conditions that were not foreseen originally. Code that was added during maintenance has its value mainly in terms of providing smooth operation and a high degree of reliability. Usually the original code provided the functionality that motivated the customer's acquisition in the first place. If that functionality had been inadequate the customer probably will move to a subsequent version. However, newer versions of the code will likely include adaptations and perfections that will motivate additional sales."

Thus, given that the positives and negatives can balance each other out, Wiederhold found that it is reasonable to assign the same value to lines of old and new code. In TSV valuation, it is reasonable to use relative code size as a surrogate to measure value of a component of software source code. If the methods to obtain metrics are used consistently and without bias, the numbers obtained will be adequate for the inherently difficult objective of valuing software for management purposes.

Significant research in software cost modeling began with the extensive 1965 SDC study[103] of the 104 attributes of 169 software projects that led to some useful partial models in the late 1960s and early 1970s. The late 1970s produced a flowering of more robust

---

[103] See citeseerx.ist.psu.edu

models such as SLIM, Checkpoint, PRICE-S, SEER, and COCOMO.[104] This dynamic field of software estimation sustained the interests of those researchers who succeeded in setting the stepping-stones of software engineering cost models and discussed the pros and cons of one software cost estimation technique versus another, which essentially provided the present analytical techniques.[105]

Two metrics are commonly used in estimating cost projections. They are, Lines Of Source Code (LOSC), and number of Function Points. In using these metrics to help compute value, the various aspects of programs can easily be measured once the software is at a version release milestone. One can look at Lines Of Source Code or the number of Function Points. In counting Lines Of Source Code, it is important to not count comment lines[106], which should be ignored, and multiple lines for a statement should be counted only once. For Function Points, software modules that appear multiple times should likewise be counted only once. If modules are written in multiple languages, conversions must be made. There is function-point literature available that provides tables that relate function points to code for many languages.[107] Common procedural languages have ratios of about 100 Lines Of Source Code per Function Point, while Visual Basic is rated at 35 Lines Of Source Code per Function Point. However, Lines Of Source Code may be

---

[104] Software Development Cost Estimation Approaches – A Survey, Barry Boehm, Chris Abts University, Sunita Chulani IBM Research
[105] ibid
[106] However, as found by DSI, commented source code, if not in escrow, had a large negative validation factor, that played heavily on the verification and purpose of the analysis.
[107] Jones, C. (1997), Applied Software Measurement, Jones, C., 1997, McGraw Hill.

the most useful for valuation purposes as it was the most common metric used for costing purposes.[108]

An input requirement for either algorithmic model is a metric measure of the size of the finished system. In COCOMO, lines of source code are used, which is obviously not known at the start of a software project. However, in software inventory source code valuations, the number of lines of source code or source lines of code (SLOC) can be easily determined. Likewise, consideration should be given to the fact that SLOC is dependent on the programming language and environment and should be analyzed within the relevant constraints in the valuation. It should be noted that KLOC, or 1000 lines of (source) code, is typically used in reference articles instead of SLOC for easier reference. Using COCOMO to calculate a value for the source code component is a simple linear COCOMO equation to determine the number of man months. Essentially, man months = $C*(KLOC)^k$ where C = a constant and k = another constant. The C and k constants are determined in COCOMO to be based on productivity parameters and past efforts.

The COCOMO cost and schedule estimation model was originally published in 1981. It became one of most popular parametric cost estimation models of the 1980s.[109] The COCOMO II research effort was started in 1994 at USC to address the issues on nonsequential and rapid development process models, reengineering, reuse driven approaches, object-oriented approaches. COCOMO II was initially published in the Annals of Software Engineering in 1995.[110]

---

[108] ibid

[109] Software Development Cost Estimation Approaches – A Survey, Barry Boehm and Chris Abts from the University of Southern California and Sunita Chulani from the IBM Research Lab in San Jose.

[110] ibid

The model has three sub models, Applications Composition, Early Design and Post-Architecture, which can be combined in various ways to deal with the current and likely future software practices. The model used here had been calibrated to a database of 161 projects collected from Commercial, Aerospace, Government and non-profit organizations. A primary attraction of the COCOMO models is that the fully available internal equations and parameter values are available. Over a dozen commercial COCOMO '81 implementations are available; one (Costar) also supports COCOMO II: for details, see the COCOMO II website"[111]

Using other information to calibrate the software inventory's KLOC value parameter could be quite helpful to determine the reasonableness of this KLOC value. For example, beginning in 1986, Data Securities International also began to value software for debt financing under its verification service and, as part of its verification process, was able to gather information relative to code size of software product deposits in escrow. It is estimated that by 2006, the number of verifications exceed 1000 escrow software product deposit verifications of proprietary software. The data base of KLOC to proprietary software product was proprietary to Data Securities International. For other nonproprietary software one could also look at open source projects that pertain to assets of similar function to determine reasonableness of relative size. For example, by March 2014, the SourceForge repository claimed to host more than 430,000 projects and had more than 3.7 million registered users in SourceForge[112] alone.

---

[111] http://sunset.usc.edu/csse/research/COCOMOII/cocomo_main.html.

[112] SourceForge is a web-based service that offers software developers a centralized online location to control and manage free and open-source software projects. It provides a source code repository, bug tracking, mirroring of downloads for load

Software costing models generally require estimates of effort and duration. In using the costing model to estimate the software inventory value, the main input is usually the software size. Effort prediction models take the general form of effort = p*S where p is a productivity constant such as one SLOC per man month and S is the size of the system. For this example, once the value for p is known, one could calculate the cost of the effort.

An example is to use COCOMO II to compute an example of the anticipated cost. For a hypothetical Ultra Lite Unix Data Base Management (ULUDBMS) software product that had 8500 lines of source code at first version release. In this example, 28.9-man months was determined to be the effort by the COCOMO II engine. If we use $20,000 per month for the expected 28.9-person man month effort, then the source code component cost to replace would be $578,000.00. If the associated FASB risk factors were determined to be non-influencing[113] and the SLOC size of 8500 was also determined to be reasonable using another database information, then the TSV-OV would be $578,000,00. This value could also provide some guidance in determining the reasonableness of the actual expenses from a financial statement that might need to be attributed to the other software inventory component.

COCOMO II Inputs

---

balancing, a wiki for documentation, developer and user mailing lists, user-support forums, user-written reviews and ratings, a news bulletin, micro-blog for publishing project updates, and other features.

[113] Comments in the source was not included in the equation. But, are very important in the management analysis.

	Equivalent Size (SLOC)
New	8500
Reused	0
Modified	0
Total	8500

COCOMO II Outputs

Top-level Estimate for Elaboration and Construction

Effort	28.9 Person-months
Schedule	10.7 Months

Activities (effort in person-months)

	Effort (Person-months)	Schedule (Months)
Inception	1.7	1.3
Elaboration	6.9	4.0
Construction	21.7	6.7
Transition	3.5	1.3

In the example above, $578,000 was the TSV-OV COCOMO II calculated management value for this inventory component. One could also determine the reasonableness of this estimate using both the actual financials provided as well as other costing methods such as the SLIM model described above. However, source code is just one of the items in the software inventory group. Each item in that group should have a corresponding identification and value component. A TSV-OV value for an open source project, would need to be adjusted by any missing internal components required for the diffusion stage and appropriate CIF risk factors.

Software developed for commercial use can be valued for a variety of purposes and, under FASB No. 86, treated as an asset by the corporation. The risk and quality influencing factors for a TSV-OV valuation are technology feasibility, management commitment, financial feasibility, ownership statements, and intellectual property rights. If these factors are computed to be less than one, they would weigh negatively on any TSV-OV value proposition, as would missing components for commercialization.

A valuation factor still missing from software cost replacement valuations is the time factor. This factor may be something discussed in the future by the experts.

> Editorial note: "I had heard many times in discussions of the valuation method of cost replacement for fair value or ownership, that once software was developed, time would be of no consequence in the re-build valuation and lost revenue was not an issue. Thus, only the costs to replace were of sole importance. Many of these comments came from advocates not in the software product area and could not comprehend that for a company to rebuild, time lost to market a product with lost revenue was not a factor they should consider. For some fair market valuations, one needs to comprehend that for some software products, it takes years to build. One might refer to the IBM book on developing an operating system. Called "The Mythical Man-Month". The book is essays on software engineering and project management by Fred Brooks first published in 1975, with subsequent editions in 1982 and 1995. Its central

theme is that "adding manpower to a late software project makes it later". This idea is known as Brooks' law and is presented along with the second-system effect and advocacy of prototyping. So, is the value of having the product the same as having the product sometime in the future. What is lost by not having the product now? In some valuations the concept of lost revenue is appropriate. I believe for certain software valuations; the time factor needs to be considered."

In completing a software inventory's TSV-OV, all components should be calculated and analyzed to yield a total software inventory value. The individual values for each of the software inventory components provide financial and management governance.

For example, let's assume we had identified and valued all the intellectual asset (IA) components of Ultra Lite Unix Data Base Management (ULUDBM's) software inventory and computed the TSV-OV fair value of ULUDBMS to be $1,400,000.00. We now can use this value in other situations such as determining a software patent's value for licensing or sale. Let's assume for discussion, we wish to value a software patent that was associated with ULUDBMS.

In this example, let's use the rule of thumb patent valuation that was explained in a 1999 LES article by Bob Bramson.[114] The article discusses a rule of thumb for a patent value to be $V = p.v.(X*Y*Z)-\$$. One could consider this equation of use to illustrate the TSV-OV

---

[114] Rules of Thumb: Valuing Patents and Technologies, LES Nouvelles, December 1999

benefit of the software inventory in a patent valuation for a carrot[115] licensing scenario. In Bramson's rule of thumb; V is the patent value, p.v. is present value, X is the percentage likelihood of commercial success of the software product, Y is the applicable royalty or license rate, Z is the applicable royalty/license base over a period of years, and $ is the cost of completion of development. Using Bramson's rule of thumb, for carrot licensing of a software patent, or software embedded in a physical product, the owner must decide whether a patent royalty or a software license will be used to define the Y parameter. Assessing the value of X for a software product is easier in some ways and harder in others. X might depend on the stage of the software product. It is well known that, if a technology owner is willing to spend the incremental cost of advancing the technology one or two levels closer to the diffusion stage, the value that the owner receives will increase dramatically and probably more than justify the increased investment. Thus, one could assume that at a minimum the TSV-OV could decrease the cost to development $. If so then, the new equation is simply $V = p.v.(X*Y*Z) - \$ + TSV(OV)$.

To conclude, it is important to remember that one of the most significant issues in dealing with valuation of software components, especially for monetization purposes, is that much of software components are trade secrets and need to be managed as such in the valuation. For those components of patents, trademarks, disclosed copyrights and industrial design, federal registries exist and incorporate legislation to protect the owners and investors in these types of assets. The risk to a meaningful valuation of this type

---

[115] A carrot license is a license to practice a patented invention that is entered into amicably, while a stick license is often the result of a Patent Infringement Lawsuit that resulted in the infringer of the patented invention agreeing to license the patent in question.

is probably not significant because for intellectual property claims and marks are identified and can be registered.

For the non-disclosed and non-registered remaining software inventory there are disclosure risks that need to be managed. The risks could be significant as the non-disclosed inventory is usually not deposited (registered) with any governmental organization. Data Securities International (DSI) was able to mitigate disclosure in the valuation as the evaluation and valuation were to the source code on deposit in the DSI private archive/registry. For any question on the content of the component valuated, DSI could simply reexamine the components deposits[116] in its private registry. To manage meaningful valuations for trade secrets it may be best to deposit the trade secrets in a private and secure registry for the holding of the components. This should also help a business to assert ownership, maximize monetization, invite investments, and receive fair calculations of value for these assets.

---

[116] A DSI level 3 verification validated many of the components of Table 4 and were required for collateral valuations.

Chapter 7

Market value of software

Traditional market valuation[117] metrics that apply to physical technology may not always adequately work for the valuation of software components. Since the value generating principles such as identification, possession, ownership, and trade secrecy for software can be lost easily by failure to take the appropriate due-diligence measures. Some software management best practices and thoughts are highlighted in Exhibits B-D. Such thoughts discuss the need for an intellectual property audit and a private registry to give assurance that the value principles of ownership, possession, trade secrecy and privacy are being maintained and risk managed.

---

[117] Market value or OMV (Open Market Valuation) is the price at which an asset would trade in a competitive auction setting. Market value is often used interchangeably with open market value, fair value or fair market value, although these terms have distinct definitions in different standards, and may or may not differ in some circumstances. See Wikipedia for market value

A software product is a complex bundle of assets and consists of both intellectual property (IP) and intellectual asset (IA) components. The components of intellectual property comprise patents, trademarks, copyrights and industrial designs as these four intellectual properties have legislation to govern, protect, and protect value propositions for the legal owners[118]. The other components or intellectual assets (IA) would then be considered to include trade secrets, know-how, and other the tangible descriptions of specific knowledge which a software business uses to support commercialization. Software, by virtue of its component inventory can be the subject of various valuation strategies. For example, if there are patents involved then the statutory rights granted can be used:

- to value a given patent,
- to generate monopolistic income via a license program of that patent,
- to allow strategic value activities such as cross licensing, or
- to perform an investment IP management analysis[119].

Many corporation's software product inventories contain no patents. However, if there are patents, one could consider the market value of any patents or trademarks to be independently valued from the software product inventory.

Ownership value, as mentioned, is the view of value if the owner is deprived of the ability to monetize and/or exclusively use. The concept of market value assumes that if a comparable property has fetched a specific price then the property in question would fetch a

---

[118] Intellectual Asset Identification, The First Step in an Intellectual Property Management Program, Dave Tyrrell and Gary Floyd, Vertex Intellectual Property Strategies Inc.
[119] See http://intellectualassetsinc.com/client-services/ma-analysis/

price similar to it. Estimating fair market value of an asset assumes that the transaction is not going to take place in an open market where the free forces of supply and demand are active, so in estimating fair value the owner and purchaser are conceptually brought together where the deal is fair to both parties.

The various methods employed by professionals who analyze intellectual property and intellectual assets for market and fair values are cost, market, and income-based methods. These 3 methods are the basics in valuing intellectual property assets and the experts recommend multiple valuations to reach a final determination of market or fair value. An introduction to these methods follow with a discussion of how specific software constructs could be included. According to the experts each of these methods of valuation has limitations, but together they can provide a set of very useful decision-making tools.

As discussed, a cost-based valuation model focuses on the costs incurred to develop the intellectual asset. It provides an estimate for the value of the asset that is tied to the cost to create or acquire the ownership of the asset.

Market-based valuation models for software-based patents and trademarks estimate the value by looking to the marketplace. Patents or trademarks that are comparable to those in question are identified, and the sales or transaction revenue derived from those comparable assets are used as an estimate of the value of the patent or trademark asset. When comparable IP assets can be readily identified, market-based valuation models are relatively easy to apply and can yield useful projections. Finding comparable transactions is the key to the market valuation method. This is relatively easy in the case of real property where the neighborhood, square footage, and number of rooms can be used to compare past home sales in order to value a potential home sale. Such is usually not the case for IP such as patents and trademarks as there are few public trading markets for patents or trademarks (say other than Ocean Tomo[120] and a handful of other international IP auctions), the terms and conditions of IP asset transactions vary widely, IP assets are inherently dissimilar, and the details of IP asset transactions are rarely available to the public. If it is difficult to find a comparable for a patent or trademark, it will be even harder to find a comparable for a software intellectual asset trade secret component.

A central issue for software inventory's trade secret valuation is the notion of registry. Unless software's intellectual assets are identified and registered (private[121] or federal[122]) by the owner, valuation is quite hypothetical. Software intellectual asset components are normally considered to be unpublished copyrights and trade secrets without a private or federal registry[123] or a TSV deposit[124] for identification, any valuation is certainly questionable.

Without the trade secrets registered somewhere, verified, and evaluated, what did the valuation refer to in future references. Even at the time of the valuation without disclosure? In the case of

---

[120] Ocean Tomo introduced the world's first public auctions of patents, trademarks and copyrights.

[121] www.dsiescrow.com Data Securities International started the first software escrow company in 1982

[122] http://app.legalis.net/geneve/gb/indexgb1.htm A Swiss registry associated with the EU

[123] The Agency for the Protection of Programs (APP) is a European association of software developers and information technology professionals, registered under the French law of 1901.

[124] TSV deposit is one that contains all the background inventory components.

a patent asset, claims and claim information regarding the patent are deposited and registered in the PTO. As is a trademark. A best practice for both software and trade secret valuations is to have the asset components placed in a registry such as a software proprietary escrow account. Then verified, validated, and then valued. Depositing the software component assets in a registry account by and for the valuation subject matter expert is a good way of providing an audit trail of what was valued for future reference. A best practice for an open source software valuation should be to register the components in a private registry, as any member of the open source consortium could change any component at any time in the open source site, such as "SourceForge"[125].

Factors that affect a software product market valuation comparability include: the relative balance of power between the buyer and the seller, industry concentration, market size, barriers to market entry, the growth outlook for products incorporating the commercialized software components to be valued, and anticipated new product introductions. Experts in the field of valuation of IP asset have identified four basic requirements for the market method to be functional. They are:

- an active market must exist for the asset,
- there must be enough similar asset exchanges in the recent past,
- price information on similar asset exchanges must be available to the public, and
- the exchanges must be between independent parties.

A complication for software product valuations, are that few

---

[125] http://sourceforge.net/ *SourceForge*.net: Open Source Software

software product ownership transfer transactions are ever available to the marketplace. Software products that is included in a company acquisition, are seldom apportioned from the acquisition price[126]. What we typically find are paid licenses to commercialized software products, which have little to do with the ownership, fair, or market value of software.

Income-based valuation models make use of current and forecasted future revenues to develop an estimate of an asset value and are appropriate for certain software product context valuations. In the income valuation model, the amount of license revenue that a commercialized software product could generate is used to establish the software product's market value. The Income-based models have adopted a forward-looking perspective, estimating future earnings that can be derived from commercial use of the asset. Different companies and valuators apply different definitions and projections regarding "revenue forecasting". Therefore, because of this diversity, the income-based valuation model differs, in practice, from company to company.[127] This is especially even true for software product income valuations.

Income-based models function best for software products and IP (patents, and trademarks) when there is accurate information to support future income and future cash flow projections. This information is more likely to be available when the valuation is for an asset already in the marketplace or it will reach a clearly established market. Income-based models are less effective when income and future income information is sketchy or speculative.

---

[126] See FASB 141 and 142
[127] Valuation of intellectual property rights, Ms. Namita Chandra, Paras Kuhad and Associates

Experts suggest that there are four parameters that need to be investigated for estimation on the income method. They are;

- "The amount of net income the asset is expected to generate.
- The time period over which the income is expected to be received.
- Determination of the present value discount rate for future income, and
- The risk of realizing the future income,"[128]

In estimating the net income inherent in a software product, one must estimate how much revenue the software will generate during its life. This could require estimating the assets Remaining Useful Life (RUL) factors. If the software product is licensed to others, the expected income depends on the licensing revenue or number of licenses times the license price. To value the net income also requires the risk of realizing future income. Future income is directly tied to the ability of the software to meet future obstacles.

Most software product costs are incurred during the period after the software product is first delivered to the marketplace. These costs are primarily due to software enhancements, support and maintenance. These costs refer to the activities to preserve the software's ownership and market worth by modifications, revisions and continuous improvement in functionality and performance in the marketplace. Successful software products have many versions, long lifetimes, and corresponding high maintenance cost ratios over their lifetime.[129] Software lifetimes are typically 10 to 15

---

[128] ibid

[129] What is your software worth? Gio Wiederhold, Communications of the ACM September 2006

years and even longer and are likely to increase[130].

The discount rate for future income is commonly built on future cash flow estimates associated with a particular asset. Models project future earnings and expenditures attached to the asset. The estimates are also discounted to account for the time value of money and the uncertainty as to the accuracy of the projected cash flow. The net present value of the future earnings is calculated so that the estimated potential value of the asset can be compared with similar estimates.

An issue for a software product in analyzing future income is determining operational risk. Software operational risk is the risk factor associated with migration to future technology, and issues determining systemic problems such as internal procedures and failures by people and systems to continue to deliver expected support. Many different analytical models are presently being applied to estimate the market or income value of intellectual property. In the model proposed by the article "What is your software worth?"[131] proposes an analytical model using many of the constructs discussed in his article. Although his model has its limitations, it provides an alternative to investors and financial managers to better understand the potential market or income value of software.

Another weakness common to all software valuations, without a TSV[132] deposit, is the failure to account adequately for the legal aspects of software's intangible assets, their development,

---

[130] Smith, G. and Parr, R. Valuation of Intellectual Property and Intangible Assets, 3rd Edition. Wiley, 2000
[131] Gio Wiederhold, Communications of the ACM September 2006
[132] Total Software Value (All inventory components necessary)

protection, and transfer. To account for those legal aspects effectively, the valuation models should include estimates or actual costs associated with a legal audit and opinion of the ownership, possession, and other rights in any market or fair value analysis. This audit should go hand and glove with any encumbrance audit of licenses to the software product.

The central constructs for software product valuation should be the identification of the software inventory components, the possession or registry access by the corporation, and the ownership assignment statements. These are the primary constructs to keep in mind for software valuation. An important point to remember in market valuations of a software product, is, only after the market has been established and demand is apparent, the software inventory contains the only assets with any value. After the market is established current and future revenue of the software product will again be dependent upon these same intellectual asset components. The quality of the software inventory will play an important part in future fair and market valuations of software.

Chapter 8

Software trade secrets value.

Wikipedia defined computer software as:

> "anything but hardware, meaning that the "hard" are the parts that are tangible while the "soft" parts are the intangibles inside the computer. Software encompasses an extremely wide array of products and technologies... Software is [also] involved in video games and the logic systems of modern consumer devices such as automobiles, televisions, and toasters."[133]

With such diversity how can management ever begin to understand software value? Total Software Value's (TSV)[134] came into existence by Data Securities International to help solve this dilemma.

The opportunity or need to value a trade secret is quite common

---

[133] http://en.wikipedia.org/wiki/Computer_software; Overview
[134] Software and Valuation in the Information Society, LES Nouvelles, June 2008

when an organization decides to not patent a software-based invention, but rather to harness the invention exclusively within the organization. This need may be the case when an entity decides to develop computer software internally to automate certain processes for cost savings instead of license-in software a and then request the owner to customize it. This may also be the case for providing software-based services on the internet as a Cloud software service.

The TSV-ICS valuation context was specifically developed by Data Securities International, Inc.[135] for owners of software-based trade secrets to understand the value propositions of their trade secrets in their custom software[136]. Custom software is generally defined as any software that is developed and or modified for some purpose. Software that is licensed-in and then modified by the owner or customized is not the focus of this article for it violates the TSV value generating principle of ownership.[137] The focus of this chapter is on software developed by the entity, for the entity and ownership vested with the entity for the trade secret.

The valuation analysis using TSV for just trade secrets has two parts, the software inventory value analysis and the use value analysis. At first read, one could consider TSV-ICS confusing or badly named for this trade secret context, however this context was initially called TSV-ICS, by DSI, for the Internal Cost Savings or revenue potential

---

[135] http://en.wikipedia.org/wiki/Data_Securities_International
[136] Custom software is computer software that is specially designed for a single person's or a small group of persons' specific needs. Custom software includes modifications to canned software and can be developed in-house by the user, by outside developers, or by both. Washington Administrative Code WAC 458-12-251.
[137] See Software and Valuation in the Information Society, LES Part 4 September 2009

that could be generated by a trade secret. For example, did the internal development, internal use commercialization and then use of the trade secret generate software asset value of cost savings or revenue or both?

In valuing a software-based trade secret using TSV, the TSV-OV software inventory asset value[138] and CIF[139] risks analysis should be completed first then the income method analysis for revenue or cost savings. In TSV-ICS, software-based trade secrets have both a value in the software inventory as a capital asset used to make money[140] and an internal cost savings or revenue value in the use of the trade secret. The TSV-ICS analysis attempts to deal with the complexity of the value proposition of the trade secret. The TSV-ICS value is the revenue derived or cost saved in the use of the trade secret and the TSV(OV) value is the asset value of the software inventory components. One could consider this like a software process patent where the market value is the net present value of the patent and the commercialization process builds additional value in the software inventory of the patent.

Any software-based trade secret is proprietary technology and confers to its owner competitive advantage relative to its competitor is generally recognized as a valuable technology intangible[141] and this is especially true for software that is built and used internally. There are numerous reasons to conduct a

---

[138] Software Inventory Valuation Part 3 – A TSV (OV), LES Nouvelles, June 2009

[139] Composite Influencing Factors

[140] In financial economics, it refers to any asset used to make money, as opposed to assets used for personal enjoyment or consumption. See http://en.wikipedia.org/wiki/Capital_asset

[141] Valuing Intangible Assets, Robert F. Reilly and Robert P. Schweihs, McGraw-Hill 1999

valuation of a software-based trade secret and in using Total Software Value (TSV) concepts there are three primary but different value contexts[142] that are highly appropriate to consider in software products. These three different analyses were developed to value the different contexts and associated risks of software owned by an entity for the entity. The three contexts provide insight;

- for managing the software inventory (OV),
- for a market sale of the trade secret (MV), and
- for trade secret Internal Cost Saving (ICS).

Consideration by the trade secret software product owner of these distinct contexts helps with insight into; governance, investment, sale, exclusive licensing, Cloud use royalty management and apportionment. Consideration of these contexts also helps the stockholder, stakeholder, or investor with transparency into the software trade secret assets owned by the company.

Custom software products of trade secrets may be least understood outside the entity, but undoubtedly has an enormous impact[143] to the entity. In valuation of trade secret software, it is important to know the context;

- Is the question what did the entity pay to build the trade secret software? Or even
- Is the question what would it take for the competition to build the trade secret software and how long?

As mentioned earlier, some software valuations use the cost to

---

[142] Or framework; A set of assumptions, concepts, values, and practices that constitutes a way of viewing reality.
[143] The Economic Valuation of Trade Secret Assets, R. Mark Halligan, Esq., Richard F. Weyand

replace method. In the cost to replace a trade-secret based software product using this method, the analyst can use historical expenses to cost value the custom software product. This process can yield good valuations when the historical data was accurately captured as true expenses for the all software components. But if the historical expenses were not accurately captured or may be unreasonable, then this could yield questionable valuations. The TSV based valuation identifies each software inventory component and then gives to management or the investor what the experts say is the reasonable cost value to recreate the custom software product inventory components. In some cases, the TSV influencing risk factors are informative besides the value potential. TSV software valuations that use cost replacement projections of all the components other than historical book value data, may have more transparency for investors and stockholders.

Central to a TSV-ICS valuation are the same TSV value generating factors of; identification, possession, and ownership. Identification, possession, and ownership are key to a TSV trade secret value and additional background on trade secrets might be quite helpful. From the article "The Economic Valuation of Trade Secret Assets"[144] a discussion of the legal aspects of trade secrets was quite important in the application of valuation principles.

> "A trade secret can only be validated in litigation. Until there is a judgment entered in a civil lawsuit that the Plaintiff possesses a trade secret, there is no legal trade secret status. In contrast, there is a presumption of validity when patent, copyright and trademark certificates are issued by the Unites States government. An official

---

[144] ibid

certificate defines the specific intellectual property right that exists. Trade secrets, however, remain inchoate and subject to the vagaries of the litigation process. The burden of proof is on the trade secret owner to show the existence of a trade secret as Plaintiff in a misappropriation lawsuit. The Plaintiff cannot rely on presumptions flowing from a prior *ex parte* examination by the federal government.

There are four proofs required to prevail on an assertion of trade secret protected status in court:
> - Existence. The information must qualify as a trade secret asset.
> - Ownership. The plaintiff must be able to prove ownership of the information.
> - Access. The plaintiff must prove the defendant had access to the information, that is, that the defendant did not independently re-invent the trade secret.
> - Notice. There must be actual, implied or constructive notice of the trade secret status of the information prior to the misappropriation.

Failure of any of these four essential proofs puts the trade secret assets at risk."[145]

What is a trade secret? A widely relied-upon definition of a trade secret:
> "trade secret may consist of any formula, pattern, device or compilation of information which is used in one's business, and which gives an opportunity to obtain an advantage over

---

[145] ibid

competitors who do not know or use it. It may be a formula for a chemical compound, a process of manufacturing, treating or preserving materials, a pattern for a machine or other device, or a list of customers."[146]

A trade secret is usually distinguished from a patent either because:

- it consists of something that cannot be patented;
- it consists of something in the process of being patented (and still secret); or
- a decision was made that keeping the product or process as a trade secret because it was more beneficial to keep secret than seek a patent.

In order to claim the benefits of trade secrets as intellectual property or in the event of stolen trade secrets, trade secret owners must have an estimated value for the trade secret to assess value or damages for civil liability or criminal prosecution. One of the following three methods (from the U.S. Department of Justice's Task Force on Intellectual Property in their Progress Report of the Department of Justice's Task Force on Intellectual Property) may be used to find an estimated value:

- Cost to develop the trade secret;
- cost of acquisition; or
- fair market value if sold.

The understanding of the legal aspects and how they may impact any valuation is quite important as just noted. The items below help identify the software inventory components usually associated with "internally commercialized" custom software for trade secrets. These items help give identity to the trade secret software components that are owned by the entity, and all should

---

[146] Restatement of Torts, Section 757

be considered proprietary, valuable, and all managed as trade secrets. When done, a better understanding of what Karl Jorda hints to in his comment "Patents are but the tips of icebergs in a sea of trade secrets.... patents have value and possibly more valuable are the background assets."[147]

Internal Commercialized Asset Inventory Example

Employee as User Support Systems	R&D Components
Installation and training	Internal Design Documentation
User documentation and help	Source code with comments
Appropriate databases	Source code control with comments
QA and testing	Databases
Bug/support system	**Internal Commercialization**
Testing code and data	3rd Party software
Manufacturing System	QA and System software and tool base
Specific build guides	Executable systems
Strategy	IT Support documents
Software enhancement plan	
Employee as User Support Systems	

If TSV-ICS is the view of value for the use of the trade secret, then how might the use be valued? What are the value propositions of the trade secret apart from the cost to replace value? Many intellectual property transactional valuations use a net present value (NPV) of income to value a technology that is generating revenue or saving costs, this can also be true for trade secrets. If the trade secret is generating revenue or saving costs, then valuation can be done using the standard income method of valuation to derive an appropriate value proposition for use of the trade secret. In using the income method, one must determine the

---

[147] The Differences between Patent and Trade Secret, Franklin Pierce Law School, Summer/Fall 2004

appropriate contribution for the trade secret in order to determine a net present value for a trade secret investment. Here the contribution could be the historical or anticipated difference in revenue income with the trade secret vs. without the trade secret.

In net present value analysis, the income method adopts a forward-looking perspective, estimating future earnings that can be derived from the use of the trade secret. Currently, different companies and valuations apply different definitions and projections regarding 'revenue forecasting' with most forecasting based upon the present value of the expected income to be earned from the technology trade secret in the economic model. Because of this diversity, the income-based valuation model differs, in practice, from company to company. One might consider for trade secret valuations when using the income method, that the remaining useful live (RUL) from the TSV-OV software inventory analysis could be quite useful in helping determine an appropriate projection period. For example, if the RUL factor is low, that is the current software inventory is quite limited in technical transportability[148] then the projection period should reflect a more limited period.

TSV-OV is the value and analysis of the trade secret's software inventory created during the research, development and internal commercialization of the idea, process, or method using software computer-based technology. This analysis can be done any time in the "internal commercialization phase" but is most informative when the trade secret-based software product is in use. For example, if this is at first use, then we have a value context of the first version of the software inventory. Caution should be taken to

---

[148] See http://en.wikipedia.org/wiki/Abstraction_layer and Part 4 - Software Valuation –TSV(MV), LES Nouvelles September 2009

only value those software inventory capital assets that have identity and exist in digital form. For example, if an inventory component is the reference document for use and exists on the internal website, the TSV value is in the cost to re-produce the digital document not the cost to copy a document or maintain a website. The value emphasis is on the digital inventory, not the cost to Xerox copy or house it.

The TSV-OV uses the costing model, such as COCOMO, with CIF risk analysis, to analyze and value as many of the software inventory components as possible. A historical or typical cost can then be used to value any remaining inventory components. Historical cost should be examined for reasonableness. TSV-OV analysis considers the cost to recreate each software component like the original software component. In future analysis to recreate the component, certain CIE[149] influencing factors should be examined to determine to what extent the re-created component might adjust the corresponding cost value of the original component. For example, if the new component is technically better than the original software component because it "contains" or is built with "newer" software technology, then this could impact the asset value of the inventory component. This factor is like the obsolescence factor discussed in many software valuations, but in TSV-OV this factor is analyzed for software not the hardware upon which it resides. Methods used to depreciate tangibles as well as intangibles assume that the goods being valued lose value over time. Such depreciation schedules are based on wear, the loss of value due to obsolescence, or changes in customer preferences[150]. However, well-maintained

---

[149] CIE – importance or exception factors
[150] What Is Your Software Worth?, Gio Wiederhold, Communications Of The ACM, September 2006.

software, in active use, does not wear out, and is likely to gain value[151].

In the TSV-OV analysis of TSV-ICS, the valuation analyst should use an appropriate software engineering costing model such as SLIM, Checkpoint, PRICE-S, SEER, COCOMO[152] or Function Point Analysis[153] as a basis to calculate the anticipated cost to recreate inventory components such as the source code. The costing model will yield a reasonable indication of how long the experts say it will take in types of technical manpower and number of man months to recreate the component. The type of manpower and time can be multiplied using standard labor costs to yield a replacement cost value of the component. However, this may still not give appropriate credit to the trade secret's special components.

Currently, all the International Standards Organization (ISO) for costing methods such as for function point counting, measure the relative number or size of software functions, similarly to COCOMO's number of source code statements. For example, in the function point counting method, the intermediate algorithmic transformations, translations and conversions of data types are not included in the measurement.[154] The reason given for not considering algorithms in the model is because there are no internationally accepted ways of defining or quantifying their complexity. However, for most applications, complex algorithms only exist in a very small proportion of the software. A commonly accepted way to address the impact of the algorithms is to isolate

---

[151] Spolsky, J. Joel on Software. Apress, 2004.
[152] Software Development Cost Estimation Approaches – A Survey, Barry Boehm, Chris Abts University, Sunita Chulani IBM Research
[153] http://en.wikipedia.org/wiki/Function_point
[154] ibid

the functional area and apply a different cost factor or analysis to those areas that have complexity. This possible imbalance may be corrected by additional costs of more senior consultants or experts. However, the use of even more senior manpower may not be a total solution. In TSV, it is extremely important that the analyst give appropriate cost value credit to the research and internal design components. The expert analyst must be careful to value these special invention complexities.[155] These components will "house" the first embodiment of the invention or idea. In the analysis for ownership value the expert analyst must consider a reasonable research time required in order to prepare the internal or/and functional design documents. Caution should be done as these are extremely valuable documents and highly confidential as they are the valorization[156] of the trade secret(s). It may take considerable expertise[157] to determine the reproduction cost. In TSV-OV the cost value analysis is for a reasonable reproduction that does not mimic the component in analysis, but rather re-invents the component using different experts than the original inventors.

In software valuation of a software product with patents using TSV-OV, the idea that a product's software inventory asset value could be considered additive to a software product patent's value proposition in certain situations. The example used a patent's present value formula, in this case a 'rule of thumb' patent value

---

[155] Complexity can be interpreted into four categories: problem complexity, algorithmic complexity, structural complexity and cognitive complexity. Information Technology Journal, Volume 7, 2008

[156] In modern translations of Marx's economic writings, the term valorization (as in French) is preferred because it is recognized that it denotes a highly specific economic concept. It refers both to the process whereby a capital value is conferred or bestowed on something, and to the increase in the value of a capital asset. See http://en.wikipedia.org/wiki/Valorisation

[157] For some research, as at the University, solutions may have taken years.

formula, proposed in a 1999 LES article by Bob Bramson[158] where the TSV-OV value could be added back to the patent's value as component of the commercialization effort. Likewise, for a trade secrets TSV-ICS value, the trade secrets TSV-OV could also be considered additive to the trade secrets TSV-ICS value.

A goal for software based intellectual property professionals should be to help identify and value software based proprietary technology that confers competitive advantage. Such a goal will give management insight into governance, investment, sale, exclusive licensing, licensing royalty management and apportionment. Such a goal will also give stockholders and investors transparency into the software assets owned by the company.

The concept of a Total Software Value (TSV) deposit was developed by Data Securities International (DSI) in the mid 1980's to value software to provide some internal corporate governance, debt financing, and to help protect stakeholders of risk mitigation where possible for their trade secrets.

> Editor Note:
> The following is an example of one of DSI's technology escrow services. A stakeholder (angel investor) invested money in a small company that was developing new software products. The stakeholder requested DSI to escrow and validate the trade secrets being developed. This proactive act by the stakeholder saved the trade secrets from being taken when the developer wanted to exit the company with the software assets in question. The

---

[158] Rules of Thumb: Valuing Patents and Technologies, LES Nouvelles, December 1999

escrow secured the stakeholder's equity and enabled it to maintain ownership interests in the current developed components of the software. Further, the escrow helped show there was enough documented information for the courts to decide that the developer could not take the software and bankrupt the company. In the mid 1980's many software-based companies had a difficult time explaining to stakeholders and angel investors[159] the value of the software developed by the company. In the evolving digital world, the transparency and value of software for an investor is largely still missing.

TSV-OV discussed the analysis for valuing the software inventory for ownership value. A TSV-OV ownership analysis includes replacement cost valuing all the components in the inventory. It can also be used for the valuation of an open source product (more on the in a later chapter). The ownership value of software is in the ownership of the software inventory of a proprietary software product. Although open source software is often called "free to use", it is still in all most cases "proprietary", meaning that someone still owns the software inventory and deserves credit for

---

[159] An angel investor (also known as a business angel, informal investor, angel funder, private investor, or seed investor) is an affluent individual who provides capital for a business start-up, usually in exchange for convertible debt or ownership equity. Angel investors usually give support to start-ups at the initial moments (where risks of the start-ups failing are relatively high) and when most investors are not prepared to back them. A small but increasing number of angel investors invest online through equity crowdfunding or organize themselves into angel groups or angel networks to share investment capital, as well as to provide advice to their portfolio companies.

its development and subsequent uses[160] and sale[161]. When including open source in the software product inventory, companies can protect the value of closed-source, trade secrets, patents, copyrights and their trademarks, by classifying open source (especially Free and Open Source Software, FOSS) into buckets or classes based on license restrictions.[162]

---

[160] Living with Open Source: Implementing, Managing, And Enforcing A Uniform Policy For Your Enterprise, LES Nouvelles, September 2009
[161] January 16, 2008 Sun Microsystems, Inc. (NASDAQ: JAVA) today announced it has entered into a definitive agreement to acquire MySQL AB, an open source icon and developer of one of the world's fastest growing open source databases for approximately $1 billion in total consideration
[162] ibid

Chapter 9

Software assets as collateral

In Gordon Smith's book "Valuation of Intellectual Property and Intangible Assets", third edition, he discusses that proprietary technology or trade secrets and know-how is often more valuable to an enterprise than its patents. He references Karl Jorda, David Rines Professor of Intellectual Property Law and Industrial Innovation at Franklin Pierce[163] who states

---

[163] No law school in the world has had an impact on intellectual property law and infrastructure like UNH Law. Our Franklin Pierce Center for Intellectual Property prepares the next generation of lawyers for practice in a global economy based primarily on intellectual property. https://law.unh.edu/centers-institutes/franklin-pierce-center-intellectual-property

"Patents are but the tips of icebergs in a sea of trade secrets. Over 90% of all new technology is covered by trade secrets and over 80% of all license and transfer agreements cover proprietary know-how or hybrid agreements relating to patent and trade secrets."

Much of those trade secrets are in software processes, products and programs, electronic databases maintained by software, and trade secrets embodied as software. With so much invested in software how can it be leveraged, e.g. used as collateral?

Relatively few organizations appreciate the full scope and flexibility available to them in terms of unlocking the asset in their software. Typically, a company seeking financing is looking to expand, acquire another company, refinance or cover seasonal shortfalls in working capital. One of the most overlooked methods for utilizing the value of software was its use as collateral. This activity, however, is becoming more common as the importance of proper intellectual property and intellectual asset management gains recognition and as increased cash flows associated with the licensing of intellectual property and assets catches the eye of Wall Street.

There are several other reasons why a software owner might be interested in pursuing this kind of strategy. First, it can provide a method for transferring some of the risk associated with receiving future software licensing revenue. If the financing is non-recourse[164], the risk of receiving the license payments is transferred to the lender.

---

[164] https://financial-dictionary.thefreedictionary.com/Non-Recourse+Finance
Non-Recourse Finance. A loan secured by the revenue of the project the loan intends to fund, and nothing else. That is, non-recourse finance does not allow the bank or other lending institution access to the borrower's other assets in the event of default.

Second, it may increase the return on the software through increased leverage. This is because the present value of impending license streams is being collected in a lump sum today rather than spread out over the future. This lump sum payment can then be invested in current projects that feature an internal rate of return that is higher than the cost of the financing. Any upside potential residing in the software is typically retained by the software owner as well. Third, and possibly the most important, is it provides a source of capital that does not dilute the current equity structure. With venture capital discounts typically in the range of 25% to 50%, this is very beneficial when compared to equity sources of financing, especially for smaller technology companies. An additional benefit of this kind of financing is that the interest payments may be tax deductible. This helps to offset a portion of the discount taken as a result of the present value analysis.

Software products as assets fall into one of two categories:
- those with specifically identified cash flow from licensing ('Cash Flow Software') and
- those with implicit value [165](Implicit Software').

Cash Flow Software are typically software product or imbedded software in physical components that are licensed and producing a revenue stream. With these assets, the license and royalty payments from the license agreements are attributable to the licensed software product or software component. Implicit Software assets include trade secrets, unregistered copyrights, and software components that are not licensed, marketed or used only internally.

---

[165] implicit value here is meant that the only value is in the current software inventory.

While many high-tech companies invest in Implicit Software, there are few instances of financial institutions lending against software without accompanying license streams. Usually only Cash Flow Software will generate interest from lending institutions. This is because the two primary concerns for the lender are that the funds loaned are secured by "license revenue" collateral and that there is enough cash flow available to service the loan payments.

With Cash Flow Software, there are several aspects of this kind of financing that are important to understand. First, the financier is primarily interested in the cash flow:

- How long has it taken place? Has it been consistent?
- Is it growing?
- What are the potential obstacles that may arise?

Because the lender is focused on the cash flow and the likelihood of being repaid, it is the credit rating of the licensee(s) that is of importance, not only that of the software owner. The licensee(s) is/are the ultimate source of the cash flow that will be used to repay the loan. In fact, a small entrepreneur that licenses software to a large stable corporation with a great credit rating is likely to get a more favorable interest rate than a more established software owner that licenses to an organization without an exemplary credit history.

Second, lenders will prefer the software assets of a small software company reside in a wholly owned subsidiary that has a totally separate operation from the software owner. Referred to as a Special Purpose Vehicle or Entity ("SPE"), these holding companies serve to protect the lender against the possibility that the software owner will file for bankruptcy protection. If there is not a SPE already in place, setting one up will be one of the first steps taken.

Third, a trust account will likely be required. Unlike other loans with which you may be familiar, the trust account will remain a vital part of the payment activity throughout the life of the financing. The mechanism is straightforward. All royalty payments made by the licensee are paid into the trust account. From these proceeds, the amount required to service the loan is paid to the lender. Any funds beyond that are paid to the SPE, which may then use them in the management of the software or intellectual property or may pass them on to the software organization.

Finally, the due diligence agenda associated with this kind of financing is likely to be much more extensive than other lending activities. It will likely consist of legal items such as title searches and software ownership and patent validity, financial items such as valuation and cash flow verification and analysis, and technical items such as obsolescence potential, current and potential competition, and product life cycle. All of these will have to pass a thorough inspection before the financing will go forward.

When financiers lend against Implicit Software or when the license stream is not enough to cover the loan payments, lenders will need to understand the implicit ownership value of software and mechanisms to secure the software should the lender have to foreclose on the loan.

First, an ownership valuation with proprietary escrow usually comes with an objective, to evaluate the software components, prepare a valuation, and secure the components for the loan. Obviously, in the past most lending organizations were typically reluctant to accept software as a surety. As we know, for an asset to be acceptable collateral to a lending institution, the asset must be identifiable and transferable. Other conditions are usually required for software to qualify as a basis for financing, as well. A bank would like there to be a market for the technology with an ongoing revenue base of existing clients and the software must be functionally maintained at an acceptable competitive level. In addition, the rights necessary to complete ownership transfer, and the proper materials for use in ongoing maintenance and development, must be readily retrievable and transferable.

In an article written by Priscilla A. Walter when she was at Gardner, Carton & Douglas, a Chicago law firm, titled 'Leveraging Intellectual Property Assets' the means of documenting security interests in intellectual property are described.

> "These procedures and the collateral preservation procedures enable the lender, in the event of default, to convey the company's assets intact to a third-party purchaser."

The purpose, of course, is to maximize the value of the software, to the advantage not only for the secured lender but also for the other creditors of the company and its shareholders. A necessary step in preserving the value of software is to make sure the software will be available for use, immediately and easily, in the event of a default. It does little good to have an assignment of the copyright in the related proprietary software if the lender does not have immediate access to an up-to-date copy of all required components the software inventory this will include internal documentation. Rights to copyrights on computer software are to little avail without related engineering and production software and clear documentation as to which software components are used with other software to create a releasable and usable product.

To complement this article, Candace M. Jones, a Partner at Hahn

Loeser & Parks LLP, wrote 'The Changing Nature of Collateral: Security Interests in Intellectual Property' for the February 2000, University of Dayton Law School Licensing Intellectual Property Seminar titled 'Intellectual property. What is it? How do lenders take and perfect security interests in the intellectual property assets of their borrowers?' Then John F. Hornick at Finnigan wrote

> "Intellectual property owners seeking loans may find that their most valuable property for use as collateral is their trademarks, copyrights, or patents. In fact, a bank that provides capital or credit to an I.P. owner will most likely require that the I.P. owner's intellectual property assets be pledged as collateral. Most banks will insist on obtaining a security interest in the I.P. owner's trademarks, copyrights, and patents using a security agreement that greatly favors the bank and may severely restrict the I.P. owner's ability to alienate any of its intellectual property assets in the normal course of business.
>
> For a lender to obtain priority over other parties who might have interests in the I.P. owner's trademarks, copyrights, and patents, the lender must perfect its interest in the intellectual property. One perfects a security interest by filing the right documents in the right place. The perfection of security interests generally is governed by the Uniform Commercial Code (U.C.C.) as adopted by the states. However, the ownership of trademarks, copyrights, and patents generally is governed by federal law. As a result, uncertainty has arisen as to which body of law—federal or state—governs the perfection of security interests in trademarks, copyrights, and patents."

The framework for analyzing implicit software as collateral is substantially the same as the analysis for any hard asset of a borrower. First, the lender must identify the software owned by its borrower and determine the ownership value of the software. Then the lender must cause security interests to be attached and be perfected. Finally, the lender should take certain steps, including obtaining certain rights in its security agreement, that will aid in the enforcement of its security interest should the borrower default on its obligations. Software products are potentially protected by four types of intellectual property legal rights: patents, trademarks, copyrights and trade secrets. Some intellectual property rights arise under federal law, and some are created by state law.

Similarly, federal law provides some of the rules regarding perfection of security interests in certain forms of intellectual property, while Article 9 of the Uniform Commercial Code, as adopted by the states, controls in other circumstances. The combination of state and federal laws complicates the process for obtaining and perfecting security interests in intellectual property.

These insights point up one the idiosyncrasies of software: one must have access to both a physical manifestation of all the inventory components of a software product and the underlying rights to it in order to exploit it. Thus, Data Securities International helped developed another type of escrow, valuation, and audit processes called 'Software Collateral Escrow' (SCE). An SCE was used to implement the requirements outlined above. An SCE account set up with an intellectual property escrow or trust company, provided the lender with access to all parts of the software asset used as collateral against a loan default. The SCE escrow deposit contains the source code, documentation, firmware, schematics and any other components that the lender needed to secure the technology as collateral. Such SCE account should be verified, validated, and valued. This collateral escrow process and valuation analysis helps eliminate any ambiguity about what the borrower really owns and what it might be worth if there is a default on the loan. To assure the lender of its position if the software is covered under copyright, the escrow agreement should include the ability to execute a Copyright transfer document. This document will allow the lending institution to take ownership of the technology under default conditions. This is the same process that applies when a bank repossesses a car if the buyer defaults on a loan.

An implicit software product valuation provides interesting challenges to the intellectual property appraiser. For any intellectual property valuation company, determining an accurate fair market value of the software in a going concern is difficult enough because it requires an accurate forecast of future revenues and earnings of the company whose software is being valued. However, the lender is not simply interested in the value of the software in the context of a going concern, but in the context of a hypothetical future liquidation as well. This compounded the difficulty of determining a reasonable liquidation value for the software without understanding the makeup of the software for future value.

Intangible assets such as software are usually valued at fair market value. Fair market value is the value of an asset to be sold in an arm's length agreement where there is a willing seller and a willing buyer. An asset in liquidation, however, is sold under distressed circumstances, which tend to complicate the typical arm's length transaction. In liquidation, there is usually a severe discount in value from the fair market value of the software in a going concern. With little history to fall back on, the intellectual property valuation company must find new methods to calculate the liquidation value of software that at the time of valuation is still active and viable. It becomes even more imperative that the valuation analysis look at the ownership value of the software as well as its market value. One might look at Federal Accounting Standards Board regulation FASB No. 86 as an aid in understanding software as a financial asset prior to license revenue.

Traditional hard asset appraisers have a distinct advantage over intellectual property appraisers as hard assets have a long history of being liquidated in distress sales. There is extensive data available on the amount of discounting which could be expected for any class of asset sold in liquidation. Conversely, very little data exists on the value of individual intangible assets being sold in liquidation. Usually the intangibles are sold as part of a company sale and, until the changes in standard accounting practices, there was no separate accounting of intangible asset values from the overall goodwill booked in the transaction.

Chapter 10

Thoughts on open source; it's not free!

How do you put a value on free to use open source? That's was 'the' question facing investors of open source software enterprises. Few doubted that open source enterprises were shaping the software landscape. Open source products are based on various open source licenses and are developed by global open source communities. In some cases, they were giving proprietary software enterprises a run for their money.

The clear language of the 'Artistic License'[166] created conditions to protect the economic rights in the granting of an open source

---

[166] The original Artistic License was written by Larry Wall. The name of the license is a reference to the concept of artistic license. Whether or not the original Artistic License is a free software license is largely unsettled.

software (OSS) license[167]. These conditions govern the rights to modify and distribute computer programs and files included in an open source downloadable software package. The attribution and modification transparency requirements directly serve to drive traffic to the open source incubation page and to inform downstream users of the project, which is a significant economic goal of the copyright holder that the law will enforce. Through this controlled spread of information, the copyright holder gains creative collaborators to the open source project; by requiring that changes made by downstream users be visible to the copyright holder and others, the copyright holder learns about the uses for his software and gains others knowledge that can be used to advance future software releases, open or proprietary.

A word of caution, since the underlying software of open-source companies is free to use, Matt Asay[168] suggested analysts wonder if they were worth multimillion-dollar valuations from investment funds and big-name suitors. At one time, fans of the open-source movement saw signs of froth. Matt Asay raised an important issue:

> "is most of the money going into open source, dumb money? Not dumb in terms of the VCs funneling the money to startups, but dumb in terms of the business thinking underlying the startups?"[169]

---

[167] Different licenses allow programmers to modify the software with various conditions attached. According to the Black Duck KnowledgeBase, a database of some two million open source projects, five of the most popular licenses are: MIT License, GNU General Public License (GPL) 2.0, Apache License 2.0, GNU General Public License (GPL) 3.0, snd BSD License 2.0 (3-clause, New or Revised). When you change the source code, OSS requires the inclusion of what you altered as well as your methods. The software created after code modifications may or may not be made available for free.
[168] See CNET's The Open Road blog website
[169] CNET's The Open Road blog website

Then again, Kim Polese[170], stated that the deals might not make sense using traditional valuation benchmarks.[171] The old assumptions about return on capital might not apply when it comes to open source. Most users don't pay for the product's use. At the same time, the collaborative nature of open source cuts development and marketing costs. Open-source firms have a phenomenal user base and can be a disruptive force that can potentially be worth a lot of money.[172] Yet, it seemed obvious that open source enterprises that make friends, but no money would end up in the same bankruptcy as failing proprietary software enterprises. But maybe not!

Palamida Software (now Flexera)[173] and Blackduck Software[174], are two companies that provided products and services to software enterprises that co-mingle the use of open source with their proprietary code. They believed enterprises were increasingly mixing internally developed code with external code from the open source community and other third-party suppliers.[175] This practice was a huge productivity multiplier, and according to Blackduck, when managed poorly, mixing code can introduce significant business issues.[176] Un-managed use of open source and other non-owned proprietary code, if ever detected, could open the door for copyright infringement, patent validity issues, or generally be catastrophic for the enterprise executives. Such undisclosed use will cause significant errors in any proprietary software inventory

---

[170] CEO of open-source firm SpikeSource
[171] ibid
[172] ibid
[173] https://info.flexerasoftware.com
[174] https://www.blackducksoftware.com
[175] EBiz "Black Duck Software Launches Open Source Code Center" 01/28/2008
[176] ibid

valuation or market valuation, especially if part of the valuation is based on lines of source code.

According to Blackduck,

> "application development has evolved into a process of assembly. As developers are writing their code, they capitalize on software reuse by finding software components already written that enhance their projects. Such development techniques are legal—the reused components are available within open source applications and libraries, or developers use third-party components that have been acquired by their employers."[177]

When managed correctly, by legal counsel and executive management who set policies regarding use of open source and 3rd party proprietary code, then appropriate governance of the software product is possible with a more accurate valuation. Assuming the open source or third-party components can be detected or extracted from the software inventory, then the appropriate software inventory valuation TSV-(OV) with any market valuation TSV-(MV) can consider the governance risks and influencing valuation factor of open source use.

For companies that have already taken steps to comply with the open source licenses to which they are subject, the CAFC's decision in Jacobsen[178] should not have a significant impact (see below). Jacobsen had the potential to significantly increase the risk of noncompliance with open source licenses. For those companies that have elected not to comply with open source licenses or, as is the case with many companies, have chosen to remain unaware of

---

[177] ibid

[178] Jacobsen v. Katzer was a lawsuit between Robert Jacobsen (plaintiff) and Matthew Katzer (defendant), filed March 13, 2006 in the United States District Court for the Northern District of California

the open source software licenses to which they may be subject, Jacobsen should be all the incentive that is necessary to adopt and implement a sound open source license compliance program.

"On August 13, the Court of Appeals for the Federal Circuit (CAFC) issued its decision in the Jacobsen v. Katzer case. This case was the first real test of the remedies for breach of open source licenses in US courts. Unfortunately, the District Court decision was wrong and wrong in a way that could have been a disaster for open source community. The District Court found that the requirements in the Artistic License for notice were merely a contractual covenant rather than a condition on the scope of the license (the courts sometimes use the word "restriction" on the scope of the license and "condition" at other times, but they have the same meaning). Consequently, under the District Court's analysis, Katzer's actions were not copyright infringement. Thus, Jacobsen was limited to the traditional remedy for breach of contract, monetary damages, rather than the copyright remedy of injunctive relief (injunctive relief means that the court will order Katzer to comply with the terms of the contract). The CAFC reversed the District Court's decision and its reasoning is very helpful for the open source community. The court found that the limitations in the Artistic License were "conditions" on the scope of the license and, thus, Katzer was liable for copyright infringement (as well as breach of contract). The CAFC noted that the Artistic License imposed its obligations through the use of the words "provided that" which is generally viewed as imposing a condition. Although the reasoning is limited to the Artistic License and the interpretation of each open source license will depend on the wording of its provisions, this decision is a welcome change to the District Court decision. The case has been remanded for the District Court to determine if the other criteria for injunctive relief have been met, but the CAFC's decision strongly suggests that they have been met. The open source community should thank the lawyers who worked hard and on a pro bono basis (i.e. free) to achieve this victory."[179]

Open source software valuation (See Chapter 11) needs the help and support of financial and software business professionals to adopt and implement a sound open source license compliance program. Software management can create and maintain a functional database of the enterprise's software asset inventory to report correctly software assets. In the past the software asset inventory database was rarely available, because management had not demanded it. Today, there exist models available for implementation by information technology[180] professionals, supported by computing technology that can help alleviate the information gap and support IP valuation professionals, economists, and accountants in their critical corporate mission to provide financial software asset valuation information. Naturally, valuation of open software is largely based on experts' assumptions and estimations. The objectiveness of these assumptions is sometimes questioned. That is, the main reason for the difficulties of conservative accounting to cope with the recognition of such assets in financial reports. However, it is unrealistic to not recognize the role and governance of software assets in the functioning of enterprises in the information economy.

---

[179] See https://opensource.org/node/360
[180] the technology involving the development, maintenance, and use of computer systems, software, and networks for the processing and distribution of data.

Chapter 11

Valuation of Open Source (OSS) – it's not all free beer!

How do you put a value on free? That's was the question facing investors in and business owners of open source software. Few doubted that open source and open collaboration were reshaping the business landscape. Many believed there was only one open source landscape and it was 'free beer' for everyone. However, those who believed that there was only one model called free beer, missed some very important aspects of value in the open source movement. It is very important to remember OSS (Open Source Software) is not FOSS[181] (Free Open Source Software) and should not be confused with each other. For any information on FOSS, the reader may wish to surf the internet with the key word 'FOSS' and 'free open source software'.

In Open Source Software, when there is no direct revenue or

---

[181] That is, anyone is freely licensed to use, copy, study, and change the software in any way, and the source code is openly shared so that people are encouraged to voluntarily improve the design of the software. Wikipedia on FOSS

income from the OSS product, valuations are undoubtedly a challenge. Is open source like the dotcom bubble? If so, what caused the dotcom bubble to burst?

"During the dotcom craze, it didn't matter if an Internet company was making money or ever had any intention of reporting a profit. The fear of missing out was huge. IPOs helped create millionaires overnight and sent the NASDAQ to record levels. Like all economic cycles, it had to end. But no-one really expected it to end so dramatically. With the wisdom of hindsight, we can see that the steam was taken out of the bull market. In the early part of the 1990s, the Fed lowered interest rates to combat the recession, making it cheaper to borrow money. A familiar tale. What venture capitalist and investor doesn't like to borrow cheap money and throw it at a start-up or red-hot stock market? Again, it doesn't matter if a dotcom stock is making money, is saddled with debt, and has nothing to take to market; the potential was there. But the economy never stands still. Annual GDP increased throughout the 1990s and, from 1997 to 1999, hovered around 4.5%. In an effort to help moderate economic growth, the Fed started to raise interest rates. From 1999 to early 2000, the Fed raised its key lending rate six times.

But what exactly caused the dotcom bubble to burst in 2000—or, at least start seeping air—on March 10, 2000? No one knows why stocks started to retreat on that day. No doubt, analysts attributed it to a slight correction. The effects of the dotcom bubble were felt around the world. Amidst all the static and economic discussions, what we do know is that investors finally clued into the fact that the Internet companies with nosebleed valuations that they

invested in weren't making money and were saddled with debt. Moreover, Internet companies looking for new capital found it difficult to attract new investors. Higher interest rates didn't help. Investors ran for the exits, and once-high-flying Internet stocks started to go broke. On March 10, 2000, the NASDAQ hit an all-time intra-day high of 5132.52. The September 11, 2001 terrorist attacks put an end to a decade of growth. On October 9, 2002, the NASDAQ bottomed at 1114.11, having lost 78% of its value."[182]
This is not the case for open source.

Traditionally, copyright owners sold or assigned their copyrighted material in exchange for money. The lack of money changing hands in open source licensing should not be presumed to mean that there is no monetary or economic consideration. There can be substantial benefits, including monetary benefits, to the creation and distribution of copyrighted works under public licenses that range far beyond traditional license royalties. Even for an individual program creator who may generate market share by providing certain components free of charge. Similarly, a programmer may increase his/her national or international reputation by incubating open source projects.

Valuation methods and principles may or may not be the best method or analysis factors to determine the value of any potential OSS investment transaction. Companies and individuals looking to have their OSS acquired or to be funded through venture investment must be familiar with current practices of valuation as well as possible OSS methodologies and principles. It will be

---

[182] www.lombardiletter.com/market-crash-what-caused-the-dotcom-bubble-to-burst-in-2000/9162/ and en.wikipedia.org/wiki/Dot-com_bubble

especially important for the OSS owner to be prepared to defend any proposed asset value discussions and OSS monetization models.

For example, one common OSS monetization model is 'the corporate enterprise directed open source development'. This is where a corporate American company (European or pick a country) invests in open source software development to achieve a business objective. Some suggest this business model is based on selling proprietary complements to free open source software. This OSS model is quite proprietary and any characterization as 'nonproprietary' is certainly surprising. For example, IBM uses this model to sell IBM hardware, ancillary software and service with open source software and generated billions of dollars of revenue.

Another monetization model is the 'open-source-hybrid' model where companies have 'tweaked' their business models to provide certain software free (including the source), but other software only available as part of a payment scheme. For example, a PC based single user version may be 'free beer' but access to the enterprise version is only available when you purchase a license. This 'open-source-hybrid' model also offers a similar and efficient model to the 'proprietary' free trial before purchasing a license.

There are many reasons why any enterprise would opt for an open source model or collaboration and forego the possibility of making or investing in only the proprietary licensing route. As mentioned earlier, some OSS companies gain profits in other ways than direct revenue license gains. Others suggest the reasons include:
- cost savings, in terms of zero investment,

- productivity gains, as more and more people will be able to access and try the usage,
- brand building, since more and more people will be-come aware of the product in the markets and,
- most importantly, an expanded user base.

As the OSS market expands, revenues from sales, one-off licenses, dual licensing, and complementary products and services maybe enough to offset the direct revenue opportunity of open source. IBM had used this approach very successfully. Many companies use some type of open source software, and one can assume many have plans to use it in the future. Utility and telecommunications firms, media companies, and public sector bodies led the enterprise adoption by a wide margin. European firms had been actively adopting open source solutions over the past many years. At one time, almost 40% of companies had already use some type of open source software. At that time Forty-five percent of the firms using open source have deployed it in mission-critical environments, although the vast majority (70 percent) used it for non-key applications.[183]

The terms of the Artistic License 1.0 were at issue in a 2007 federal district court decision in the US which was criticized by some for suggesting that FOSS-like licenses could only be enforced through contract law rather than through copyright law, in contexts where contract damages would be difficult to establish. On appeal, a federal appellate court

> "determined that the terms of the Artistic License are enforceable copyright conditions"[184].

---

[183] Is Open Source Gaining Adoption in Europe? Forrester', Manuel Ángel Méndez
[184] ibid

The case was remanded to the District Court which did not apply the superior court's criteria (on the grounds that in the interim, the Supreme Court had changed the applicable law). Regarding legal OSS enforceability issues, as has been widely publicized in the industry, legal and even mainstream media, on August 13, 2008, the U.S. Court of Appeals for the Federal Circuit (CAFC) issued its decision in the closely watched case of Jacobsen v. Katzer. In its decision, the CAFC confirmed one of the core legal assumptions upon which the entire open source world is based - namely that open source licenses are legally enforceable as licenses under U.S. copyright law.[185] Thus, free as well as open source has potential economic value.

OSS owners, investors, and the software valuation industry should be looking at alternative principles and methods for software valuation to augment existing mechanisms as we continue into this new information economy. With the fact that OSS and collaboration software is a reality, and alternative principles and methods which might prove quite useful as ever-more-complex investment decisions in the OSS information economy are considered.

Augmenting any discussion of valuation methods with alternative principles maybe a good idea, but, where do you start? Certainly, similar market acquisitions of open source companies would be a good place. If we look at some past open source investment and acquisitions, Yahoo acquired Zimbra, an open source email and communications suite provider, for $350 million. Yet, Zimbra only received funding from Benchmark Partners, Redpoint Ventures and

---

[185] United States Court of Appeals for the Federal Circuit, 2008-1001, Robert Jacobsen, Plaintiff-Appellant, Matthew Katzer, Defendants-Appellees, case no. 06-CV-1905, Judge Jeffrey S. White.

Accell Partners, raising $30.5 million with three rounds of investment funding. What prompted Yahoo to pay $350 million? Another acquisition was BuzzTracker, a tiny news aggregation site, for between $2 to $5 million. Then, Sun Microsystems became the owner of MySQL, the pioneering open source database system. Sun paid about $800 million in cash in exchange for all of MySQL stock and assumed another $200 million in options as part of the deal. Being aware of past OSS acquisitions and transaction values may be a start, but with some valuators still believing OSS is just another dotcom bust, more than just market acquisition similarities may be required. Maybe the number of users of the open source software might prove worthy? Then maybe the OSS inventory too might be of consequence?

Software products as well as open source software (OSS) are a complex bundle of assets and can consist of both intellectual property (IP) and intellectual asset (IA) components. As mentioned earlier, one could consider the components of IP to comprise patents, trademarks, copyrights and industrial designs because these four intellectual properties have legislation to govern, protect, and value propositions for the legal owners[186]. The other components or IA would then be considered to include domain names, trade secrets (non-provided source code), know-how, and other design digital assets. Proprietary software as well as OSS, by virtue of their component inventory[187] (or software inventory), can be the subject of various valuation strategies and discussions.

Some believe that OSS should be valued only under trademark. For

---

[186] Intellectual Asset Identification, The First Step in an Intellectual Property Management Program, Dave Tyrrell and Gary Floyd, Vertex Intellectual Property Strategies Inc.
[187] See Tables 1 and 2 below

those that do, can these be the only value principles for OSS? What if there are no trademarks per se? Does it mean that if there was is no intent to maintain a monopoly, brand the product, or modify the General Public License (GPL)[188] to include trademark restrictions, then there is no monetary value? Whoa! Maybe in some areas of technology, but certainly not open source software and open collaboration. There is a big world of open source and collaboration activities! For example, in March 2014, one open source repository claimed to host more than 430,000 projects and had more than 3.7 million registered users in a software service website called SourceForge. [189]

In preparing for release for use of an open source software product, the effort involved produces quantities of digital asset components. Some of the components will be provided under the OSS license and downloadable from an OSS website (such as Source Forge) and other digital assets may not be provided under the OSS downloadable libraries but retained by the company/individual for

---

[188] The GNU General Public License is a widely-used free software license that guarantees end users the freedom to run, study, share, and modify the software. The license was originally written by Richard Stallman, former head of the Free Software Foundation, for the GNU Project, and grants the recipients of a computer program the rights of the Free Software Definition. The GPL is a copyleft license, which means that derivative work must be open-source and distributed under the same license terms. This is in distinction to permissive free software licenses, of which the BSD licenses and the MIT License are widely-used less-restrictive examples. GPL was the first copyleft license for general use.

[189] SourceForge.net is a source code repository and acts as a centralized location for software developers to control and manage open source software development. SourceForge.net is operated by Sourceforge, Inc. (formerly VA Software) and runs a version of the SourceForge software, forked from the last open-source version available. So show the growth, as of August 2008, SourceForge.net hosts more than 180,000 projects and more than 1.9 million registered users although it does contain many dormant or single-user projects.

proprietary or other monetary purposes. The owner(s) will make the decision of which components are open and which are closed (or not available for free).

Typical Software Product Inventory Assets
Disclosed inventory assets
• Software program for user – usually in executable format
• User documentation (paper and digital)
• Access to support FAQ's
• Patents and trademarks
Undisclosed inventory assets
• R&D components (e.g. internal design documentation)
• Installation and training documentation
• Program source code with comments
• Source code control system documentation with comments
• Various databases (e.g. error corrections, licensing data)
• Error and Bug support systems
• Client support and billing
• Testing code
• 3rd party software and licenses
• Open source software and guides
• Quality assurance data and processes
• System software with software tools database
• Specific build guides for program deliverables
• Program support documents
• Software enhancement plans
• Business plans (with marketing plans)

Software governance is asset-based and has value. Software development, as well as for OSS, produce component assets; each component comes into existence for a purpose. Someone determines that the component was/is needed to achieve "use" of the OSS software product just as for proprietary software, and if sweat, in some cases paid sweat, went into their production, than the component has as a minimum, a replacement value.

An OSS replacement valuation model must focus on the costs to re-produce the intellectual asset, not the historical sweat costs, or the non-paid sweat costs. There is a value of the asset that is tied to the cost to re-create or acquire the ownership of the asset. Free downloaded software components are not owned but licensed under the OSS license. What is downloaded and used, must be used according to the OSS license. In software asset valuations it is important to identify and value all software components.

Today, as probably for the past twenty plus years, OSS software is almost always put into use with only partial functional requirements fulfilled, and then evolves over time, frequently, over very long times, as the software is enhanced, customized, adapted as new technical requirements and standards are discovered and changed.[190] One of the greatest inherent values of OSS software is its ability to evolve and adapt to new challenges through modifications, revisions, continuous improvement through open collaboration.

Most business owners today developing software or business units that develops software including some aspect of OSS may expect to find equity or debt money for financing future developments. Venture capitalists evaluate their investment opportunities based on certain criteria. It is widely accepted that the three key investment decision criteria are:

---

[190] Software Valuation Part 2, Les Nouvelles, December 2008

- management team,
- market projections and
- product[191].

In addition, venture capitalists have preferences – like venture's stage of development, its location, its industry or technology, and size of the investment required that vary between one another. This criteria and preferences are related

> "to evaluation of an investment opportunity: does the venture have potential, is it worth our time and money, and does it fit our investment strategy."[192]

Venture capitalists base their evaluation on business plan, meetings with the entrepreneurial team, and various researches.

Valuation of high-tech companies by Venture Capitalists (VC's) has been theoretically studied extensively. The value of a new venture is derived by discounting predicted future cash flows to the present[193]. The discounting factor depends on the probability of returns. Even if an enterprise has significant potential future cash flows, the risk of failure decreases its net present value. Different methodologies exist in the valuation, but all aim at answering the same question: what is the present value of expected future earnings or exit value of a company? The methods fall into four categories:

1) Liquidation value asset-based methods,
2) Discounted cash flow-based methods,
3) Options based valuation methods, and
4) Rule of thumb valuation methods.

---

[191] Tyebjee & Bruno 1981, 1984; MacMillan, Siegel & Narasimha 1985
[192] ibid
[193] FRONTIERS OF E-BUSINESS RESEARCH, 2005 Evaluation and Valuation of Open Source Software Companies: A Venture Capitalist Perspective

Companies and individuals looking for venture investment must be familiar with these current situation and valuation methodologies.

Undoubtedly for OSS VC valuations where there is no revenue or income from the OSS, then such methods may or may not be the best method to determine the value of the situation. The business owner must be prepared to defend other asset valuation discussions. If not, the business owner must aware that the valuation will typically be based on <u>real property</u> and/or <u>real income.</u> These are a far cry from the open source world!

Chapter 12

Software risks, escrow, and the Cloud

There is inherent complexity of managing risks of software assets as they migrate to the internet Cloud[194] service providers. This is not to say that software ownership and use risks are now unique to the Cloud. Unwarranted copies may exist, but this is not a new issue for the owners of software, even if in the Cloud. Digital rights management systems have been around for quite some time and will

---

[194] Cloud computing metaphor: the group of networked elements providing services need not be individually addressed or managed by users; instead, the entire provider-managed suite of hardware and software can be thought of as an amorphous cloud. See wikipedia.org/wiki/Cloud computing. Image created by Sam Johnston

operate just fine in the Cloud and can protect the disclosed software components.

There have been risks of ownership and use without the Cloud, and we will touch on some of these plus the additional complexity of these issues in the Cloud. For example, licensors have historically relied on copyright registration protection for the software. Yet, in the Cloud, this may not always be that easy. Copyright protection may only protect certain components of today's comprehensive software program inventory. Copyright protection is typically universal and used to protect from theft specific components of the software, such as the deliverable programs, and user "how to" documentation. Copyright protection provide enforcement of un-warranted copies. But what are the enforcements in the various countries for un-wanted copies that are Cloud hosted in foreign jurisdictions? The Cloud has some generally familiar computing elements (players) that include SAAS[195], PAAS[196] and IAAS[197] that

---

[195] Software as a service is a software licensing and delivery model in which software is licensed on a subscription basis and is centrally hosted. It is sometimes referred to as "on-demand software", and was formerly referred to as "software plus services" by Microsoft. SaaS applications are also known as Web-based software, on-demand software and hosted software. The term "software as a service" (SaaS) is considered to be part of the nomenclature of cloud computing, along with infrastructure as a service (IaaS), platform as a service (PaaS). According to a Gartner estimate, SaaS sales in 2018 were expected to grow 23% to $72 billion. See Wikipedia.

[196] Platform as a service (PaaS) or application platform as a service (aPaaS) or platform-based service is a category of cloud computing services that provides a platform allowing customers to develop, run, and manage applications without the complexity of building and maintaining the infrastructure typically associated with developing and launching an application. See Wikipedia

[197] Infrastructure as a service (IaaS) are online services that provide high-level APIs used to dereference various low-level details of underlying network infrastructure like physical computing resources, location, data partitioning, scaling, security, backup etc. A hypervisor, such as Xen, Oracle VirtualBox, Oracle VM, KVM, VMware

are platforms that exist in many countries around the world.

As mentioned, software is highly sophisticated and can be protected by Intellectual Property (IP) laws, but less protection and more risks may also be in store for the Intellectual Assets (IA) if they migrate to the Cloud. Legal risks such as who's laws are used, and what countries laws govern the background intellectual assets of a software product in the Cloud? As software creators devote significant time and financial resources in the software pre-commercial phase, those investments often continue long after the software's market launch and through the software products life cycle. It is a no-brainer that owners, investors, and stakeholders of software strive to protect the valuable inventory components of that software as they migrate to the Cloud. Just as for any commercialization, the rule, 'Put protection first!' applies for managing risks.

There were certain access risks that were managed, before the Cloud, in a 'classical software model' that comprises one creator (the licensor), an application (disclosed components), a license, and a user (licensee) who installed the software application (the inventory components known as the deliverables) usually on licensee's proprietary hardware. The licensor controlled the origin

---

ESX/ESXi, or Hyper-V, LXD, runs the virtual machines as guests. Pools of hypervisors within the cloud operational system can support large numbers of virtual machines and the ability to scale services up and down according to customers' varying requirements. See Wikipedia.

and form of distribution (CD[198], USB drive[199], internet download, and etc.) of the software. Both deliverables and the undisclosed inventory assets of the software were physically managed by the licensor. The licensee on the other hand usually controlled possession of the various computer hardware on which the application ran with proprietary data. This was the situation until the user wanted access to the source code (See Exhibit H) to make sure they has access to support if the licensor went bankrupt. Data Securities International founded the first software source code escrow[200] to help manage the various licensee and licensor access risks in the classical licensing model.

The risk of software access and continuity for all players, including the Cloud stakeholders, is far more complex today than it was when this 'classic software model' has changed completely as additional parties came into play and introduce new risks as possession,

---

[198] Compact disc (CD) is a digital optical disc data storage format that was co-developed by Philips and Sony and released in 1982. The format was originally developed to store and play only sound recordings (CD-DA) but was later adapted for storage of data (CD-ROM). Several other formats were further derived from these, including write-once audio and data storage (CD-R), and rewritable media (CD-RW).

[199] A USB flash drive is a data storage device that includes flash memory with an integrated USB interface. It is typically removable, rewritable and much smaller than an optical disc. Since first appearing on the market in late 2000, as with virtually all other computer memory devices, storage capacities have risen while prices have dropped.

[200] Source code escrow is the deposit of the source code of software with a third-party escrow agent. Escrow is typically requested by a party licensing software (the licensee), to ensure maintenance of the software instead of abandonment or orphaning. The software's source code is released to the licensee if the licensor files for bankruptcy or otherwise fails to maintain and update the software as promised in the software license agreement. Data Securities International, DSI was a technology escrow administration company based in San Francisco, California. Founded in 1982, the company escrowed source code and other maintenance materials for licensees. See wikipedia.org/wiki/Data_Securities_International

control, delivery, and management, shifted between the various stakeholders of the Cloud (such as Amazon[201]), wherever they may be in the physical world.

In the Cloud, the licensee's proprietary digital data may be housed in the myriad of electronic databases servers across the globe. Data in various database platforms may not be as protectable as IP, but even IP enforcement is different in different countries[202]. In the past, data was considered owned and possessed by the licensees. Historically in the 'classic software model' most corporate data were physically controlled by the software located at the corporate information technology facilities and managed by corporate information technology (IT) departments.

In the Cloud, how exactly can one guarantee access to the background intellectual assets represented by software applications if they are dispersed in the virtual Cloud? A licensor's new risk will be to ensure that the background software components will be available to access in the future if they are also managed by someone else in the Cloud. The background assets will possibly be at the various platforms 100% uptime forbearance by some stakeholder management (possibly even backups of the assets).

Corporations that use the Cloud to access their own application plus SAAS applications may have to invest millions in new and improved critical software products and the inevitable implementation into a

---

[201] Amazon Elastic Compute Cloud forms a central part of Amazon.com's cloud-computing platform, Amazon Web Services, by allowing users to rent virtual computers on which to run their own computer applications.

[202] Almost every country has its own patent law, and a person desiring a patent in another country must make an application for patent in that country, in accordance with the requirements of that country. A US patent does not pertain to other countries laws.

Cloud landscape. Often new software, even updates, must be integrated and databases reinstalled. This requires additional costs for individual adaptations, interface programming, new hardware, modifications to surrounding infrastructure, time and effort to analyze and adapt obsolete or incompatible internal business processes, not to discount training for the employees. The body of licensors, caretakers, and users each has a strong interest in mitigating their risks involved and in protecting their investments in any opportunity and capturing potential revenue. But stuff happens! Licensors' and even some Cloud providers could default on support, maintenance or other critical deliverables and they even go bankrupt. Then what?

This conflict of interest became very apparent in the late 1970 when licensors began to keep their source code secret and not to disclose it to anyone. They understood that the source code secrets were very valuable and did not want to provide their assets to their licensees. Only the disclosed components of the programs. But the body of licensees/users sought to get hold of the source code in case the licensor defaulted on obligations or even went bankrupt. Both sides had legitimate interests. If both sides persisted in this position, they would never sign an agreement. Luckily source code escrow was invented in the early 1980's to address this specific problem. Historically, without 'source code escrow'[203] the deal may have gone south or the creator giving up its assets.

As mentioned, the issues and solutions are far more complicated in

---

[203] Wikipedia - Source code escrow is the deposit of the source code of software with a third-party escrow agent. Escrow is typically requested by a party licensing software (the licensee), to ensure maintenance of the software instead of abandonment or orphaning. The software's source code is released to the licensee if the licensor files for bankruptcy or otherwise fails to maintain and update the software as promised in the software license agreement.

the Cloud. Why? In the Cloud, who is responsible for mitigating the risk for future software component access? Who, of the body of users/caretakers have any contract/license agreement at all with the actual creators of the software product? The provider in a SAAS Cloud software product may not be the owner/creator. Who are and in what country are the creator(s)? And are they the owners? Do the SAAS players license the software to the PAAS or IAAS players or do they just have an agreement to use the platform or infrastructure? Is the SAAS player the creator or is there another creator/licensor? These are the potential nightmares of the corporate licensee's IT department. Who in the Cloud of the body of caretakers are thinking of these global issues?

In order to begin to solve this multi-national Cloud issue for critical software SAAS services, it may be wise to select a team of players who can begin to provide some guidance. Possibly, intellectual property and intellectual assets legal counsel with international bankruptcy experience[204], trusted neutral third parties with international and technical escrow expertise, and the body of user's counsels would be a good start. They must construct solutions to mitigate risks for all parties' including the licensor/owner. A starting solution could be to modify the current escrow vehicle to address the software continuity dilemma as needed.

Historically, after 1988, (the enactment of Bankruptcy Code 11 U.S.C.

---

[204] As of 2020, I believe only the United States has statues to deal with bankruptcy, licensing, and escrow such as Section 365(n) of the United States Bankruptcy Code 11 U.S.C. §365(n).

§365.n)[205] and prior to the Cloud, the software escrow vehicle was a three-party constellation in which the escrow company served as a trusted bailee or SPE[206] and held the background software inventory components in digital secure custody. Similar in concept to a notaria, bank, or legal services firm which serves as trustee in physical properties and securities. But in the Cloud, the trusted bailee must have the competency to understand the total situation and to help implement a solution complementary to the underlying multi-national agreement. The team must consider all points of view, multiple jurisdictions, and mitigate the risks including technical and value/cost solutions. Someone needs to give an opinion as to whether the escrow and contents are valuable, appropriate, and fit for the purpose of the agreements. In the Cloud this will require the

---

[205] Some... 365 (n) If the trustee rejects an executory contract under which the debtor is a licensor of a right to intellectual property, the licensee under such contract may elect (A) to treat such contract as terminated by such rejection if such rejection by the trustee amounts to such a breach as would entitle the licensee to treat such contract as terminated by virtue of its own terms, applicable non-bankruptcy law, or an agreement made by the licensee with another entity; or (B) to retain its rights (including a right to enforce any exclusivity provision of such contract, but excluding any other right under applicable non-bankruptcy law to specific performance of such contract) under such contract and under any agreement supplementary to such contract, to such intellectual property (including any embodiment of such intellectual property to the extent protected by applicable non-bankruptcy law), as such rights existed immediately before the case commenced, and not interfere with the rights of the licensee as provided in such contract, or any agreement supplementary to such contract, to such intellectual property (including such embodiment), including any right to obtain such intellectual property (or such embodiment) from another entity.

[206] See LES Nouvelles March 2008 Leveraging Software: "lenders will prefer to have the software assets reside in a wholly owned subsidiary that has a totally separate operation from the software owner. Referred to as a Special Purpose Vehicle or Entity ("SPE"), these holding companies serve to protect the lender against the possibility that the software owner will file for bankruptcy protection. If there is not a SPE already in place, setting one up should be one of the first steps taken."

legal community, technical escrow companies and consultants to work in concert to solve the dilemma. They need to create instruments and verify, validate, and value the contents that will help solve access and continuity? Then to also address the issues of the data in the Cloud!

For the technical escrow companies, these organizations need to have internal processes with verification and possible ownership validation expertise to help counsel with the deposit components, and then be ready to accommodate regular updates, electronic or media, and possibly have an international transfer capability or partner to house the escrows in an appropriate licensee/licensor country.

In the United States, congress amended the bankruptcy code, 365.n in 1987, to permit an executory contract/license to continue after bankruptcy as well as any escrow agreement that was supplementary to the license. However, what licenses exist in the Cloud? What countries is/are the licensor homebased in? If a Cloud infrastructure component provider goes bankrupt, who is responsible?

Based on the business deal, the countries involved, the parties involved, and the risks to be mitigated, the technology escrow/bailee/SPV company and counsels, may need to modify software escrow agreements and adapt new solutions to the special situations of the international Cloud. For example, Data Securities International operated prior to the Bankruptcy Code 11 U.S.C. §365n statue change for executory contracts. They worked with US counsels to prepare instruments that could begin to solve the executory license bankruptcy issues. They developed a structure like a 'letter of credit' based on 2 x 2 party agreement structures that could act as a beginning. Though this structure was never tested in court because 365n was amended. But, prior to 1986, where a bankruptcy occurred to the licensor, with a license agreement and an escrow agreement, the source code deposit was delivered to the licensee.

> Editor DSI history note: "In one situation prior to 1986, when the escrow was supplementary to an investment collateral agreement, instead of providing the escrow contents, it provided the investor with enough information to convince the judge to render the decision that the debtor could not just walk away with the valuable software assets. Because of the escrow, the investor was able to gain an equity position in the new company."[207]

Once the contract structures are worked out, specific release conditions defined, SPV defined and implemented, content and ownership transfer process agreed upon, verification, validation, and valuation determined, then the software owner can securely transmit via encryption the initial components to the first independent software escrow/bailee/SPV company for digital safe keeping. There may be some cases where this may require a secure and encrypted transfer between independent software escrow companies in different countries, the know-how, trade secrets and source code internationally to provide legal jurisdiction. This may also require the same or a different independent escrow company to accommodate the data and database for additional escrow protections for the database owners. However, if someone provides an opinion that the international escrow is not worth implementing, a single escrow with verification, validation and/or valuation should at least be considered.

---

[207] History of Data Securities International.

A major expense of a source code (trade secret) escrow registry is in the verification, validation and/or valuation procedures besides the contract formulations. Having some degree of guarantee is of the utmost importance. One wants to make sure that what is in the escrow registry is useful, informative, and of value. This was not a trivial situation for the first technical escrow companies, yet they managed to put together various sophisticated verification process.

Data Securities International defined an internal standard for 7 levels for proprietary deposit escrows, that covered validation, verification and valuation to help alleviate the issues by the licensee. Levels 1-4[208] were for verification of use licensing:

- Level 1 assured that there was a deposit
- Level 2 assured that the deposit was readable
- Level 3 assured that the deposit could create the software program
- Level 4 assured that the deposit created software program was the same as the current version in use by the licensee for critical applications.

Verification deals with continuity of the software application for use. If the deal is only for software continuity in the Cloud, then "for use" verification may be all that is required.

> Editor Note: "For 'use' (at DSI that was a level 3) verification processes typically only deal with the ability to recompile the source code into executable code that will permit the licensee to update and make changes to the existing program. However, For 'collateral and development agreements' additional verification processes needed to be

---

[208] Levels 5,6, and 7 were for collateral and other valuation purposes

done to determine if "all" components are in escrow that provide the investor party with the ability to fulfill the intent of the agreement, such as collateral where a bank needs to collapse on the assets if a loan was not repaid."[209]

Many escrow situations are centric to development agreements, collateral agreements, reseller agreements, and co-operative agreements. However, data and other components of the intellectual assets may be required to be opinioned in addition to the source code. Of course, the software escrow registry holding company must be able to verify that the deposit can re-build the application, but what else? They must also be able to technically validate any open source issues (such as is the escrow full of open source), database schematic issues, and database retention issues. Consideration might be to also provide an opinion as to the value of the software contents. Is the software ownership transferring between countries? Are there tax implications? What else might be needed for different uses of the software? These are just a few of the questions that will need to be answered by all parties.

A correctly administered software escrow registry and agreement can be beneficial to all parties, and the most obvious advantages being:

- The critical intellectual assets of the software developer is properly protected; there is no immediate discloser of source code.
- The licensor is securing a revenue stream by licensing his software to that customer, which otherwise might not have happened.

---

[209] History of Data Securities International.

- At the same time, the licensee's investment (into this software and into his IT infrastructure in general) is protected by an appropriate risk management tool.
- Licensee's need for continuity (of IT operations) is being addressed.

There are software escrow companies, though not as widely known outside of the United States, Germany and Great Britain, that can begin to provide solid solutions for controlled access to the verified, validated and possibly valued Cloud software assets (some modeled after Data Securities International, Inc. the first software escrow company that started in 1982).

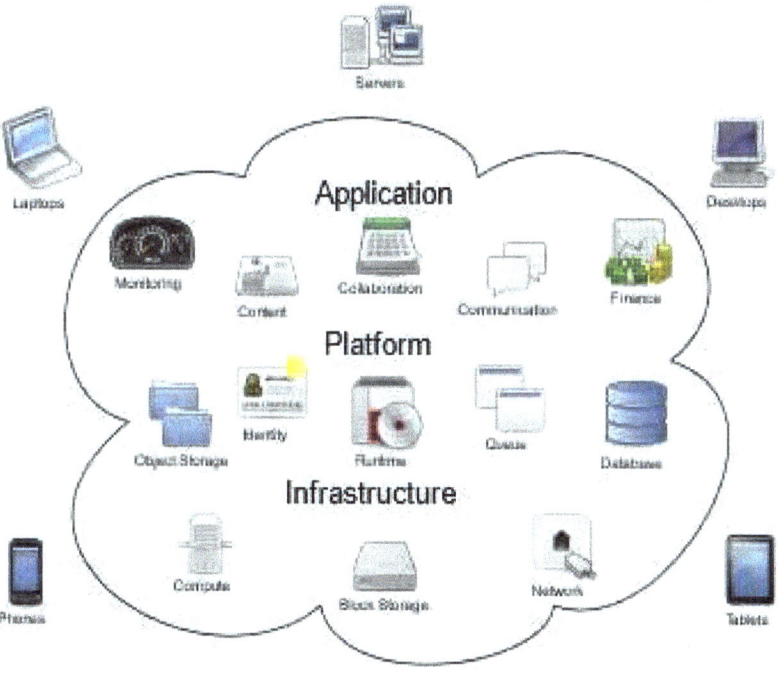

Chapter 13

Electronic records, and databases in the Cloud

Before the Cloud, data governance was done by IT personnel who were employees of the company and typically charged with the responsibilities of maintaining and securing that data on corporate computer systems. Most data resided and risks managed behind the walls of the company's data center where security, retention and backup were of primary concern. Corporate IT governance and responsible was;

- keeping data safe from migration outside the company,
- keeping the data only as long as required for legal reasons (or if vital digital records, forever),

- ensuring data consistency (its validity, accuracy, usability and integrity) and
- keeping the data backed up in case of an IT data center disaster.

These were some of the responsibilities of the IT department and to complicate these four responsibilities, data using the processes of big data, data mining, and artificial intelligence was becoming a more valuable asset and as such could be generating additional revenue directly or indirectly for the company. Thus, governance becoming more critical to the company

In the Cloud we might find licensors, licensees, providers, governments, and other stakeholders fighting for revenue without consideration of any rules of the road. Data and software that migrated to the Cloud moved responsibility for governance out of the hands of the corporation. With data and software in the Cloud, where physical are the assets, and who is responsible for governance?

Having just discussed a myriad of issues with software applications moving to the Cloud, what about the issues of digital data housed in the Cloud of various electronic databases across the globe? Data may not be as protectable as IP, but it certainly is a valuable intellectual asset. In the past, data was considered owned by the users – at least that's what they would contend. Historically most corporate data was controlled by the software run in protected information technology (IT) department; governance was done by IT personnel who were employees of the company and charged with the responsibilities of maintaining and securing that data.

In 2011 what did senior software executives predict about Cloud computing for the next three to five years?

> "One thing was clear: the software industry is in the middle of a major inflection point not seen since the client-server days. The year 2011 is already proving to be a decisive one for Cloud software and services vendors. Like a tidal force's change in direction that affects the entire Earth, there are indicators that the world of software is shifting to the Cloud. The new market reality is that—no matter their size— software vendors can no longer simply push customers to their products; rather, vendors' products need to be where their customers want to be—in the Cloud"[210].

But there was a time when Amazon struggled to restore its Web services business.

> "As technical problems interrupted off-site data storage provided by Amazon for a second day Friday, industry analysts said the troubles will prompt many companies to reconsider relying on remote computers beyond their control." "The problems companies reported ranged from being unable to access data to sites being shut down"[211]

This was a wake-up call for Cloud computing and as Mr. Lohr pointed out in his article this will be a start of the re-examination of the contracts and licenses that cover Cloud services. Can we get a handle on issues so we can help companies and clients that migrate to the Cloud, be they users or vendors?

We have over the past fifteen (15) years just begun to learn about

---

[210] www.SandHill.com , March 9 2011 newsletter, The business strategy destination for enterprise software executives
[211] Saturday April 23rd, 2011 San Diego Union article "Outage casts doubts on Cloud Storage" by Steve Lohr

the internet's potential use and dangers. We had financed billion-dollar corporations such as Symantec[212] to help fight spam, hackers, and disasters for our pc users connected to the internet. Who and what will we need to finance as the global information highway connects the Cloud infrastructure where applications and data are distributed? Who are in the Cloud infrastructure to protect data? For example, our IT departments were just learning to safely use the internet for backup of corporate pc and server data. Many have concerns about governance over these off-site archives. Even with the data encrypted and sent securely to off-site electronic backup archives.

Data backup of these new infrastructure Cloud servers will probably be of co-mingled and multiple corporate databases. If you're uncomfortable with your corporate data at an internet service provider, what about that same data backed up to Cloud electronic archives somewhere in the world? And if any backup does exist[213]! The ultimate user no longer knows where the data is housed or how many electronic archives hold the data or even how to test and restore backup data?

Fueled by the immense opportunity to use Cloud computing by the global community there needs to be a very significant wave of risk concerns. In the past, computer risk remained a constant race between increased exposure of threats on one hand and improving policies and technologies to combat them on the other. Over the past years, we've witnessed numerous business re-engineering efforts, these efforts led to higher interest levels in computer security and resulted in additional functions of computer security

---

[212] An brand of enterprise security software purchased by Broadcom Inc. in August 2019
[213] Good governance by IT was to validate annually backup data for accuracy.

applications. Examples include:

- access controls,
- electronic banking controls,
- security evaluation certification centers,
- anti-virus technology and
- distributed environments.

These advances were mostly driven by the IT departments of Corporate America who were responsible for mitigating risk of the data center. It has been said that we are entering an era of information anywhere, anytime.   The problem is that this information arena will probably include much that we do not wish to share with everyone. The full realization of this digital millennium will not come to fruition until we can conduct all our business and personal communication transactions in a secure, trusted and reliable environment.

Currently, encryption[214], and with 'public key cryptography'[215] allows for secure authenticated transactions with any party, known or unknown, with assurances of data integrity and non-repudiation of the transaction. Some of these features have been built into current internet and Cloud computing and provide a basis for the secure network needed to support electronic commerce from point to

---

[214] In cryptography, encryption is the process of encoding a message or information in such a way that only authorized parties can access it and those who are not authorized cannot. Encryption does not itself prevent interference but denies the intelligible content to a would-be interceptor.

[215] Public-key cryptography, or asymmetric cryptography, is a cryptographic system that uses pairs of keys: public keys which may be disseminated widely, and private keys which are known only to the owner. The generation of such keys depends on cryptographic algorithms based on mathematical problems to produce one-way functions. Effective security only requires keeping the private key private; the public key can be openly distributed without compromising security.

point. That is the information highway seemed secure for 'encryption cracking'[216] but for how long as new quantum computing appears to be here[217]. A primary method used to address protection of data is encryption. Users and corporations who fear the consequences of losing access to Cloud data must begin to understand who is responsible for what is happening in the Cloud to "their" secure data. For example, a simple fact from the mid 1990's was that loss of a cryptographic key used for encryption meant loss of the data. Some issue we will all watch play out as encryption is touted to solve todays Cloud privacy, are:

- who has access to a file 'decryption key'[218] in the Cloud, and?
- how fast can the codes now be broken with quantum computing?

Maybe we will have to wait for solutions to the cracking of the codes by the quantum computing world, and safety using blockchains.[219] What was learned in the 90's might also be helpful to mitigate this

---

[216] breaching of encryptions like network cracking is usually through the use of special encryption cracking software. It may be done through a range of attacks (active and passive) including injecting traffic, decrypting traffic, and dictionary-based attacks.

[217] Lightning fast quantum computers mean that we are in a new race to strengthen cybersecurity defenses

[218] encryption is the reverse operation of encryption. For secret-key encryption, you must know both the key and IV that were used to encrypt the data. For public-key encryption, you must know either the public key (if the data was encrypted using the private key) or the private key (if the data was encrypted using the public key). Symmetric Decryption

[219] A blockchain, originally block chain, is a growing list of records, called blocks, that are linked using cryptography. Each block contains a cryptographic hash of the previous block, a timestamp, and transaction data (generally represented as a Merkle tree). By design, a blockchain is resistant to modification of the data. It is "an open, distributed ledger that can record transactions between two parties efficiently and in a verifiable and permanent way".

risk as use of encryption grows with the use of a 'trusted third party' if 'key escrow'[220] is to participate in the encryption area as one solution to protecting lost access to globalized encrypted data. See also, "An escrowed encryption system can use cryptography for purposes other than data encryption, for example, user authentication, data integrity, digital signatures, key establishment, and key escrow"[221].

The huge paper conduits that have been the nerves of commerce are being rapidly replaced by computerized messages and electronic paper that also is moving to the Cloud. What in the world are we going to do if we do not have paper backup? Where will we find the originals? Using electronic records in the Cloud by replacing paper backup may make the future very different. What will be the new paper backup procedures? how will we authenticate? and will there be paper trails? For example, the validity of the computer researches notebooks, or the validity of electronic records for the patent office. Just how do we replace the paper world? Some companies have been working on these issues for years and now we will complicate the issues with Cloud based globalized digital data and records.

The current practices of using computers and having paper backups for security may have resulted in bearable risks, but what happens when all we have are electronic records? For example, in combination, USA's Securities and Exchange Rules 17a-3 and 17a-4

---

[220] Key escrow (also known as a "fair" cryptosystem) is an arrangement in which the keys needed to decrypt encrypted data are held in escrow so that, under certain circumstances, an authorized third party may gain access to those keys. These third parties may include businesses, who may want access to employees' secure business-related communications, or governments, who may wish to be able to view the contents of encrypted communications (also known as exceptional access)
[221] from "A Taxonomy for Key Escrow Encryption Systems" by Dorothy E. Denning, Georgetown University and Dennis K. Branstad from Trusted Information Systems

(See Exhibit A) require broker-dealers to create, and preserve in an easily accessible manner, a comprehensive record of each securities transaction they effect and of their securities business in general. These requirements were integral to the Commission's investor protection function because the preserved records were the primary means of monitoring compliance with applicable securities laws, including antifraud provisions and financial responsibility standards. Recent events involving Wall Street have affirmed the need to have measures in place to protect record integrity.

A close look at the USA's Securities and Exchange (SEC) Solution to records integrity maybe something that can be learned by our Cloud providers. In a letter from Mr. Michael D. Udoff[222] in 1992, of the Securities Industry Association to the SEC, he noted that until 1970, paper was the sole medium for the preservation of Broker and Dealer (B/D) records, and in 1970 the commission amended the rule to permit microfilm, and in 1979 further amended to permit microfiche. In this letter, he requested that the SEC Commission take no action if brokers and dealers maintain the required records only on optical disk storage and follow the requirements (outlined in his letter) for replacement of microfilm as backup.

In 1997, the Commission amended paragraph (f) of Rule 17a-4 to allow broker-dealers to store records electronically[223], see also Exhibit A. The rule, by its terms, does not limit broker-dealers to using a technology such as optical disk. Instead, it allows them to employ any electronic storage media, subject to certain requirements, including that the media "preserve the records exclusively in a non-rewriteable, non-erasable format." This requirement does not mean

---

[222] Mr. Michael D. Udoff Vice President Associate General Counsel and Secretary Securities Industry Association
[223] http://www.sec.gov/rules/interp/34-47806.htm#P32_4611

that the records must be preserved indefinitely. Like paper and microfilm, electronic records need only be maintained for the relevant retention period specified in the rule. See Exhibit A at the back of this article for salient parts of this ruling. Please note the bolded and highlighted sections for requirements beyond just a "backup" copy. These sections deal with duplicate, verifiable, non-destructive, audited, escrowed, and with trusted third-party access.

Electronic archiving of records and databases have similar issues to the SEC ruling. For example, one of the primary concerns is that the technology used in the future may not be compatible with current logical records and/or physical media. For example, what can you do with a 5 ¼ inch floppy disk system today? Archive (and backup) procedures for records, indexes and computer systems on behalf of a business entity is a complex issue and ideally addresses controlled access to retained materials and the audit of the corresponding software system so that the entity's electronic records are valuable and can be retrieved. In some situations, such as the SEC, the archival guidelines also must provide for an escrow agent's administrative, operational and technical system's integrity or the electronic operational structure to be highly reliable so that a copy of a deposit (or archived document) could be relied upon after retrieval, or in the event of a dispute regarding a document, for authenticity or timeliness.

Another important issue that must also be addressed is the maintenance of the sanctity and readability of the records when those records are dependent on an ephemeral technology and lost software packages. In the absence of general and widely-accepted standards for the maintenance of long-lived electronic archives, procedures, archiving of hardware and software, secure forward copying, etc., must be defined to ensure that records remain secure and readable for a specified future period and, if necessary, indefinitely. For example, a business entity that uses electronic commerce would be required to archive a variety of records/documents, will generally fall into two categories:

- journalizing the records and actions relative to the integrity, such as in the security of the system itself, and
- records of individual users engaging in their future use or protection.

There are a variety of reasons why some electronic commerce information would be archived. A few of these critical areas include but are not limited to,

- dispute resolution,
- conformance with legal requirements,
- tax audit, SEC compliance,
- banking records,
- historical purposes,
- scientific research,
- documents having continued or future legal effect, such as wills, trusts, life estates, and
- prevention of fraud (clinical and engineering testing, priority of invention and discovery).

Many issues are yet to be discussed, but some are the:

- ability to retrieve at some distant point in time,
- usefulness,
- access control,
- distributed archival,
- indexing,
- compatibility of equipment/formats,
- standards,
- archival authority, and
- quality or level of service.

For example, what did The Internet Corporation for Assigned Names and Numbers (ICANN)[224] do to protect the internet's domain names? They must have been thinking of protecting access to global "Cloud" databases and what was needed to help minimize loss of its records – that is access to all Domain Names worldwide. The current version of the ICANN Registrar Accreditation Agreement[225] ("RAA") obliges registrars to periodically submit a copy of their registration database to ICANN or a mutually approved third-party escrow agent. This escrowed data could be used by another registrar assigned by ICANN (or even temporarily by ICANN itself) to continue the provision of registrar services to the customers of a registrar whose accreditation is terminated or expires without renewal.

The Data Escrow provision is set forth in RAA subsection 3.6, provides

---

[224] a nonprofit organization responsible for coordinating the maintenance and procedures of several databases related to the namespaces and numerical spaces of the Internet, ensuring the network's stable and secure operation. ICANN performs the actual technical maintenance work of the Central Internet Address pools and DNS root zone registries pursuant to the Internet Assigned Numbers Authority (IANA) function contract. The contract regarding the IANA stewardship functions between ICANN and the National Telecommunications and Information Administration (NTIA) of the United States Department of Commerce ended on October 1, 2016, formally transitioning the functions to the global multi-stakeholder community. Much of its work has concerned the Internet's global Domain Name System (DNS), including policy development for internationalization of the DNS system, introduction of new generic top-level domains (TLDs), and the operation of root name servers. The numbering facilities ICANN manages include the Internet Protocol address spaces for IPv4 and IPv6, and assignment of address blocks to regional Internet registries. ICANN also maintains registries of Internet Protocol identifiers. ICANN's primary principles of operation have been described as helping preserve the operational stability of the Internet; to promote competition; to achieve broad representation of the global Internet community; and to develop policies appropriate to its mission through bottom-up, consensus-based processes. https://en.wikipedia.org/wiki/ICANN

[225] https://www.icann.org/resources/pages/approved-with-specs-2013-09-17-en

as follows:

> "Data Escrow. During the Term of this Agreement, on a schedule, under the terms, and in the format specified by ICANN, Registrar shall submit an electronic copy of the data described in Subsections 3.4.1.2 through 3.4.1.5 to ICANN or, at Registrar's election and at its expense, to a reputable escrow agent mutually approved by Registrar and ICANN, such approval also not to be unreasonably withheld by either party. The data shall be held under an agreement among Registrar, ICANN, and the escrow agent (if any) providing that (1) the data shall be received and held in escrow, with no use other than verification that the deposited data is complete, consistent, and in proper format, until released to ICANN; (2) the data shall be released from escrow upon expiration without renewal or termination of this Agreement; and (3) ICANN's rights under the escrow agreement shall be assigned with any assignment of this Agreement. The escrow shall provide that in the event the escrow is released under this Subsection, ICANN (or its assignee) shall have a non-exclusive, irrevocable, royalty-free license to exercise (only for transitional purposes) or have exercised all rights necessary to provide Registrar Services. "

Chapter 14

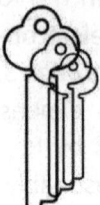

An original DSI Logo

Why software or data escrow

With the world's increasing dependence on technology and information, whether it's mission-critical software or simply a proprietary database, most companies today should be looking at improving the protection of their intellectual property assets and technology investments. One of the best ways to do so is through an effective technology escrow program. Pricewaterhouse Coopers[226] believes that intellectual property is one of the most important elements in the value of major corporations. Some analysts estimate that as much as 90 percent of the value of the world's top 2,000 enterprises in 2007 will consist of intellectual property of one sort or another. Specifically addressing software source code, Gartner Inc.[227], a leading technology research and advisory firm, has stated its belief that "it is necessary for all source

---

[226] PricewaterhouseCoopers, Building and Enforcing Intellectual Property Value: An International Guide for the Boardroom 2003, at www.pwcglobal.com.
[227] Gartner, Inc., Midsized Enterprise Summit Continuity Questions, Feb. 6, 2003, a research report for purchase from Gartner, Inc., a technology research firm, at www.gartner.com.

code to be escrowed. According to the firm, current events have created a new awareness of the importance of planning for business continuity, and technology escrow is an important part of this planning.

With some history behind the valuation of software and some introductions to the risk issues of software as an asset, then as an owner, stakeholder, or investor, you can begin to understand why technology escrow was born for the governance of software.

For example, as described by Garry B. Watzke, an inhouse corporate counsel, about investments in a mission critical application. He states "what is a practical guide to designing the right strategy for protection of the mission critical software asset. If you are talking about software, the question to ask is this one: if the software in question were gone, would its loss have detrimental effects on the productivity of your company's employees or their ability to deliver service to customers? If you answered "yes," you should consider it as mission critical software. Examples of mission critical applications include the following:

- Customer-facing technologies.
- Operational, financial, sales, and marketing applications.
- Database software.
- Server operating system technology.
- Email technology.
- Products licensed to deliver services to customers, such as portals and website.
- Partnership licensing.
- Networking, firewall, and routing technology.

Many companies already have a business continuity or disaster recovery plan in place that outlines which applications are mission critical. As in-house counsel, you may want to consider participating in the process that determines these applications; at a minimum, you should speak to the company's chief information officer to obtain the document and plan to escrow all of the applications that are on it. You can also educate the chief information officer about the importance of escrow at the inception of a software license agreement or procurement."[228]

Garry B. Watzke a past vice president and general counsel of Boston-based Iron Mountain Incorporated said in his 2004 ACC Docket 113 article "Technology escrow works like any other escrow account. Through a neutral, third-party escrow agent, a technology developer/owner places into an escrow deposit account the technology at issue, which is usually but not always software source code and any other materials necessary to allow a licensee to maintain the technology independently. If a release condition occurs, the licensee can gain access to the escrowed technology. A release condition is a circumstance under which the escrow agent would release the technology from the escrow account to the licensee. Typical release condition events are a software developer's ceasing operations or terminating support for the technology for some reason, such as bankruptcy or discontinued support of an older product. Usually signed at the same time that a license agreement is executed, a technology escrow agreement is like an insurance policy for a licensee's software purchase. Technology escrow services are a good idea when two or more parties are negotiating a license for critical technology. It provides protection of the technology for the licensee if the developer, for some reason in the future, no longer provides support. Without a technology escrow agreement, a

---

[228] Technology Escrow: Protect Your Company's IP Assets and Technology Investments," ACC Docket 24, no. 4 (April 2004): 110–123.

licensee's investment in technology is unprotected and at the mercy of the vendor. Moreover, a licensee's attempts to recover the source code and maintenance materials by other means, such as through the court system, can take years, and by then, the vendor may have already ceased operating, and resources tied to the technology lost."

In the article he commented on the legal enforceability of software escrow. "Before 1988, if a licensee found out that its technology licensor had filed for bankruptcy under Chapter 11 of the Bankruptcy Code, no legal authority supported the licensee's continued use of the technology. Thus, a bankrupt software developer could force its client to stop using licensed customer service software pursuant to the powers of the bankruptcy code. This pre-1988 situation stemmed from judicial determination that, under § 365 of the bankruptcy code, a technology license was often an executory contract, which is, generally, one in which both parties have significant obligations that remain to be performed, a description that applies to most computer software licenses and other forms of technology transfers. The bankrupt software developer (also referred to as a debtor-licensor) was allowed to reject the license as an executory contract if it would benefit the debtor to do so, and the licensee could no longer use the licensed technology. The licensee would be left with only a general unsecured claim against the developer for the damages that it suffered by reason of the developer's breach of the license agreement. The situation came into sharp focus in 1985 in the case of Lubrizol Enterprises v. Richmond Metal Finishers, Inc., one of the few cases that have interpreted bankruptcy laws in the technology licensing area. In Lubrizol, the Fourth Circuit allowed the debtor-licensor, Richmond Metal Finishers, to reject as executory its nonexclusive patent license agreement with its licensee, Lubrizol

Enterprises, for a metal-coating process. To prevent other technology licensees from suffering similar fates, Congress enacted the Intellectual Property Bankruptcy Protection Act ("IPBPA") in 1988, adding § 365(n) to the U.S. Bankruptcy Code and making technology escrow agreements signed by vendors legally enforceable under bankruptcy. The IPBPA protects the debtor-licensor's right to rehabilitate while affording the technology licensee the right to continue using the patent or licensed technology without threat of an infringement suit."

Apart from these obvious benefits, software escrow offers additional advantages that may not be so evident for the casual global observer. There are many other reasons[229].

- "First, facilitating deal closures: for the licensor, using a professional escrow service builds trust in the marketplace and thus serves as an effective sales tool. The licensor is sending out a positive market signal about his own solidity and is openly addressing the risk management needs of his customers.

- Second, fostering IP creation: Escrow generally fosters the creation of IP, more specifically by supporting the development of software, through offering more attractive market conditions – due to the additional security, licensees are more likely to buy the license from the developer.

- Third, offering additional financing options: hen looking for financing – a critical process for every software developer – software escrow offers the benefit of reducing risks to prospective investors/shareholders. A potential investor

---

[229] From Deposix.us

performing a due diligence will carefully analyze the company's IP assets and assess their individual risk. If the licensor can prove that his software is held in custody with a professional escrow service, this will add significant value to his business. And furthermore, software developers can offer to add the potential investor to its escrow as beneficiary, thereby granting them access to what typically is the major 'asset' in any (new) technology start-up.

- Fourth, improving stability in the EU for Basel II and Solvency II ratings: Escrow may help licensees to obtain a better rating under the Basel II or Solvency II schemes by reducing their overall operational IT risk, eg. failure of their critical IT systems due to a potential default of their licensor. As a result, the licensee may obtain access to cheaper credit offerings.

- Fifth, building an audit trail: From the moment of signing an escrow agreement, all events such as modifications concerning the source code are seamlessly documented and a professionally managed audit trail accumulates. The licensee will benefit from an audit trail as it allows him to roll back to older versions at any time. But also, the licensor will benefit from older versions of his source code staying in the depot of an independent trustee. In case of an IP violation, the escrow company could always prove the exact date when the licensor developed his IP, a possibly crucial aspect when it comes to patents, or cases of industry espionage or disgruntled employees which involve the IP incorporated in the source code."

Exhibit A

(From SEC 17 a-4) Preservation of digital records

(ii) The electronic storage media must:

(A) Preserve the records exclusively in a non-rewriteable, non-erasable format;

(B) Verify automatically the quality and accuracy of the storage media recording process;

(C) Serialize the original and, if applicable, duplicate units of storage media, and time-date for the required period of retention the information placed on such electronic storage media; and

(D) Have the capacity to readily download indexes and records preserved on the electronic storage media to any medium acceptable under this paragraph as required by the Commission or the self-regulatory organizations of which the member, broker, or dealer is a member.

(3) If a member, broker, or dealer uses micrographic media or electronic storage media, it shall:

(i) At all times have available, for examination by the staffs of the Commission and self-regulatory organizations of which it is a member, facilities for immediate, easily readable projection or production of micrographic media or electronic storage media images and for producing easily readable images.

(ii) Be ready at all times to provide, and immediately provide, any facsimile enlargement which the staffs of the Commission, any self-regulatory organization of which it is a member, or any State

securities regulator having jurisdiction over the member, broker or dealer may request.

(iii) Store separately from the original, a duplicate copy of the record stored on any medium acceptable under Sec. 240.17a-4 for the time required.

(iv) Organize and index accurately all information maintained on both original and any duplicate storage media.

(A) At all times, a member, broker, or dealer must be able to have such indexes available for examination by the staffs of the Commission and the self- regulatory organizations of which the broker or dealer is a member.

(B) Each index must be duplicated and the duplicate copies must be stored separately from the original copy of each index.

(C) Original and duplicate indexes must be preserved for the time required for the indexed records.

(v) The member, broker, or dealer must have in place an audit system providing for accountability regarding inputting of records required to be maintained and preserved pursuant to Sec. Sec. 240.17a-3 and 240.17a-4 to electronic storage media and inputting of any changes made to every original and duplicate record maintained and preserved thereby.

(A) At all times, a member, broker, or dealer must be able to have the results of such audit system available for examination by the staffs of the Commission and the self-regulatory organizations of which the broker or dealer is a member.

(B) The audit results must be preserved for the time required for

the audited records.

(vi) The member, broker, or dealer must maintain, keep current, and provide promptly upon request by the staffs of the Commission or the self-regulatory organizations of which the member, broker, or broker-dealer is a member all information necessary to access records and indexes stored on the electronic storage media; or place in escrow and keep current a copy of the physical and logical file format of the electronic storage media, the field format of all different information types written on the electronic storage media and the source code, together with the appropriate documentation and information necessary to access records and indexes.

(vii) For every member, broker, or dealer exclusively using electronic storage media for some or all of its record preservation under this section, at least one third party (``the undersigned''), who has access to and the ability to download information from the member's, broker's, or dealer's electronic storage media to any acceptable medium under this section, shall file with the designated examining authority for the member, broker, or dealer the following undertakings with respect to such records:

The undersigned hereby undertakes to furnish promptly to the U.S. Securities and Exchange Commission (``Commission''), its designees or representatives, any self-regulatory organization of which it is a member, or any State securities regulator having jurisdiction over the member, broker or dealer, upon reasonable request, such information as is deemed necessary by the staffs of the Commission, any self-regulatory organization of which it is a member, or any State securities regulator having jurisdiction over the member, broker or dealer to download information kept on the broker's or dealer's electronic storage media to any medium acceptable under Rule 17a-4.

Furthermore, the undersigned hereby undertakes to take reasonable steps to provide access to information contained on the broker's or dealer's electronic storage media, including, as appropriate, arrangements for the downloading of any record required to be maintained and preserved by the broker or dealer pursuant to Rules 17a-3 and 17a-4.

Hmm....

Exhibit B

A best practice for a software company M&A.

Assemble the team
Identify the software components to be valued including all IP and IA. Then assemble a valuation team. Expertise in software valuation (and validation), software registry escrow (with verification expertise), licensing and IP/IA law (depending if there are significant patents and open source to be included, more than one legal person may be required), should be assembled for the various audits and steps chosen. If the valuation is also for tax or SEC purposes, then a tax accountant should be included on the team.

Patents Involved
In merger acquisition situations, an investment IP management analysis is the first option considered when patents are involved. We recommend performing a patent portfolio landscape to help analyse either the market area or market areas ancillary to the primary market. The Investment Company or Acquisition Company should review the results to provide insight into additional opportunities.

Trademarks involved
Typically, at the roll out or early stages in the life cycle of a software product, any trademark value would be of minimal value, except for protection value of the product name. The monopoly of trademark will distinguish the product, for good or bad, as the product gains momentum in the market. However if the software product has significant market penetration then a separate investment analysis may be considered for additional

opportunities.

Copyrights involved

For proprietary products, this protection is for those user-released components to protect against unwarranted copies. If the software product is an open source product, then a careful analysis by the IP Audit team to determine if there is enough coverage for the product strategy.

Exhibit C

Investor surety thoughts

What might the process be for effectively ensuring investor surety access to the physical embodiment and preservation of software asset investments. The examples are illustrative of that process employed for investments in computer products. The essential steps are:

1. Establishing investor security for financing ownership in intellectual property by validation, valuation and verification of the subject matter of a software proprietary product, database, or website.
2. Registration when or where necessary of the intellectual property for ownership securitized purposes.
3. Digital retention of the subject matter in the appropriate form under conditions ensuring the continuing integrity of such.
4. Managing periodic updates with appropriate validation, valuation and verification of the integrity of the original and updated subject matter.
5. Collateralizing for securities purposes the registration and access to the "proprietary deposit", including additions, subtractions, changes etc.
6. Controlling registration of subject matter for investor, or other party in the same or in the appropriate form that constitutes a verifiable exact reproduction of the original (or as modified).
7. Verification of the subject matter using technology verification mechanisms for a software product.
8. Validation of the subject matter using mechanisms that designate ownership.

9. Valuation of the subject matter using mechanisms outlined by FASB 86 preliminary work constituting capitalization of software developed products.

Exhibit D

Collateral risk thoughts

I.   Software collateral escrow - Traditionally through an arrangement, commonly known as software escrow, the owner can furnish the investor with access to trade-secret materials in the event bankruptcy or similar situation. Escrow arrangements, however, have offered only limited solutions for security investments. Banks and other "investor agents" typically lack governmental infrastructure, physical access, valuation, verification, and technical means to ensure that the intent of an investment in an intellectual property investment agreement is secured. An example would be a bank's repossession of a house when the mortgage loan is defaulted requires a sophisticated infrastructure from title registries, UCC registrations, real estate valuations, and etc. The new knowledge economy currently lacks similar mechanisms for verification, validation, valuation and registration of a soft intellectual property investment.

II.   The Legal Structure - The traditional legal form of IP investments have typically used an investment document which addresses the investment and possibly a software deposit escrow, but none of the complexities of valuation, validation, or verification for the benefit of the investor who must "securitized" and "monetize" the loan. Which IP mortgage filing and what does it represent without some form of registration?

III.   Governmental Administrative Procedures - Copyright and Patent provide mortgage mechanisms to "collateralize" what may be patented or copyrighted, but trade secrets and other knowhow maybe lost. The Copyright Office requires deposit of either object code or the first and last twenty-five pages of the source code to provide registration of Copyright, and meaningless for software where the source code and other problematic technology is required. US patents are provided a mechanism to mortgage the patent at the USPTO. But this is not a total solution, only a first step to solve the investor dilemma in a software product investment. What does an investor do when the software product is not totally covered by patent disclosure and process? The patent mortgage provides only access to the claims and patent ownership, and not any background intellectual property.

IV. Financial Situation - FASB 141 requires the valuation of intellectual property investment by proper allocations, but, traditional methods do not provide any form of proper intended risk managements for a securitized investment in intellectual property.

V. Private/Commercial Administrative Procedures - There are few acceptable standards which provide validation, verification, and valuation protection for software intellectual property investments and its subsequent risks. There is no universally acceptable administrative procedure which an investment entity can use or perform collateralizing ownership interests in IP. One of the most critical areas of proof in establishing the right to damages in any such investment in IP matter is the capacity to be able to measure, quantitatively and qualitatively, that which is the subject matter of the investment.

Even the most diligent of procedures established to achieve the required standard of investment protections need reliable independent corroboration. When the intellectual property assets are intangible and involve software, the loss of any significant portion or the misuse of such may have drastic consequences. Consideration should be given to having the verification, validation and valuation by an independent source.

Exhibit E

Accounting for the Costs of Computer Software to Be Sold, Leased, or Otherwise Marketed (Issued 8/85) - Summary[230]

This Statement specifies the accounting for the costs of computer software to be sold, leased, or otherwise marketed as a separate product or as part of a product or process. It applies to computer software developed internally and to purchased software. This FASB project was undertaken in response to an AICPA Issues Paper, "Accounting for Costs of Software for Sale or Lease," and an accounting moratorium imposed by the Securities and Exchange Commission precluding changes in accounting policies related to computer software costs pending FASB action.

This Statement specifies that costs incurred internally in creating a computer software product shall be charged to expense when incurred as research and development until technological feasibility has been established for the product. Technological feasibility is established upon completion of a detail program design or, in its absence, completion of a working model. Thereafter, all software production costs shall be capitalized and subsequently reported at the lower of unamortized cost or net realizable value. Capitalized costs are amortized based on current and future revenue for each product with an annual minimum equal to the straight-line amortization over the remaining estimated economic life of the product.

This Statement is applicable, on a prospective basis, for financial statements for fiscal years beginning after December 15, 1985. The conclusions reached in this Statement change the predominant practice of expensing all costs of developing and producing a computer software product

---

[230] https://www.fasb.org/summary/stsum86.shtml

Exhibit F

Uses of Software Valuation

Acquisition Financing - In many business acquisitions, the value of computer software is an important consideration in guaranteeing either cash-flow based or asset-based financing. In some tax cases, the valuation of computer software may directly impact the refinancing or recapitalization of an established business, outside the realm of an acquisition or transaction.

Debt Financing – In many situations the tangible assets such as receivables, plus intangible patents and trademarks are not enough in value to cover or secure many investment transactions. This may be for leveraged buyouts (LBO's) or other for smart investors who want additional security. Some investors may wish to lock software asset ownership to the company verses having them taken by employees should bankruptcy conditions occur.

Business Sale/Purchase - The valuation of computer software plays an important role in the overall valuation of an enterprise. Obviously, an overall business valuation is an important consideration in the determination and negotiation of a business purchase or sale price. Plus, because computer software is typically a depreciable asset, such as under FASB 86 for federal income tax purposes, its asset value may have a greater impact on the overall business value than other assets which may not generate tax amortization benefits, such as the going concern's value of "goodwill". (See also FASB 141/142.)

Management Stewardship - The valuation of computer software and its impact on the overall business valuation may be an important consideration on the periodic assessment of the effectiveness of management's stewardship of business assets.

Intercompany Transfer Pricing - In many firms, computer software is developed by a centralized headquarters staff, and internally developed software systems are used by the various divisions and subsidiaries. The appropriate intercompany transfer price for the use of software should be a direct function of that asset's value. Depending on the relative locations of the firm's branches and subsidiary operations, nationally or internationally, the transfer price for the use of internally developed computer software can have both Federal and State tax implications. For example, outbound transfers of software can raise difficult issues for U.S. corporations that transfer software ownership to a foreign subsidiary that then transfers the ownership to another lower-tier foreign subsidiary.

Gifting Programs - In taking advantage of the annual gift tax exclusion, family business owners can transfer beneficial interest in the firm's computer software to various family members. Based upon a type of licensing arrangement, the company will retain the use of the software while the owner maintains direct equity control.

Estate Planning - In many cases where computer software is a material asset of the business, periodic software appraisals will help determine the value of the business equity and the value of the business owner's estate. Even if the business owner does not implement gifting or other wealth transfer programs, these periodic appraisals may also allow the business owner to plan for long term tax considerations.

Exhibit G

TSV Valuation request for information

Request for Information for Software IP/IA Monetization

The following information request helps provide a more efficiently analysis of the monetization, evaluation, or valuation of a software-based technology. Anyone and everyone involved in the software group should weigh in on any of these topics to contribute relevant data.

Many of these questions pertain to a Total Software Valuation (TSV) software inventory evaluation and valuation analysis which looks at the bundle of the various software components called Intellectual Property and Intellectual Assets that make software usable as a product.

GENERAL QUESTIONS & ISSUES

1. What is the history and time-line of the development of this software?
- a.   Why was this project originally undertaken?
- b.   For what specific purposes or applications was this software developed?
- c.   Is this completely new software?
- d.   If yes, then changes/enhancements to what software product or system?
- e.   Provide a time-line of important events or milestones reached.
- f.   Is development continuing or halted/finished?
- g.   Do you have documented or estimate of the programming costs?

    h.   Can you provide the number of lines of source code?
    i.   Current stage of software (proof of concept, prototype, field release?
    j.   Is this an internally implemented only?

2. Descriptions of the software, uses and capabilities.

a. Would the software...
    i.   be a stand-alone product for sale
    ii.   be a component of another system, product, or service for sale
    iii.   for use solely by the owner

b. A detailed technical capabilities and functional specifications of the software
    i.   Internal design or specification documents
    ii.   External specifications

c. Degree of custom design is necessary for each customer (e.g., proprietary custom built, vendor installs then customizes, user self-customizes, user installs out of the box as is, etc.)

d. External capabilities exist?
    i.   OLE? DDE? ODBC?
    ii.   Internet/intranet enabled through standard browser?
    iii.   File import/export (e.g. Excel, Word, Outlook, Project, others)?
    iv.   Data conversion (e.g. Access/SQL Server, Oracle, XML/XBRL, others)?

e. What platform(s) is the software based (e.g., C++, VB, Java, gnu/gcc, others)?

f. Operating systems and/or development tool kits supported

  i.   Windows, Linux, UNIX

  ii.   What would be required to implement on another O/S?

 g.   Tool kits

  i.   Development (install, compilers, etc)

  ii.   Installation (sequel, oracle, etc)

h. Cross-platform

  i.   Development vs Target System/OS

  ii.   Microcode developments

  iii.   Re-engineering requirements

    1.   the user changes or

    2.   upgrades operating systems

    3.   base interpreters

3. Third parties, open coloration, open source, free open source?

  a.   any independent companies as co-inventors

  b.   any co-inventors

  c.   any other copyrighters

  d.   joint ownership, license or use rights to any other software

4. Federal government rights (FAR) or University rights to this technology?

5. Encumbrances to

  a.   Transfer

  b.   License

  c.   Use or

  d.   Dispose of the software and related intellectual property/assets?

6. Detailed listing and description of all the technology assets that comprise the entire portfolio to be valued for licensing or sale and its current status.

> a.   Patents issued, applications, and planned applications in the U.S. and in all foreign patent offices: WIPO, etc.
> b.   Trademarks, Domain Names
> c.   Know-how associated with the software
> d.   Background technology not specifically described in the patent filings (e.g., functional capabilities, implementation techniques, compatibilities with other products, etc.)
> e.   Patents or applications that have been abandoned?
> f.   Copyrights (include open source if applicable)
> g.   If Trade Secrets (identify without disclosure)

7. Detailed additional intellectual assets

> a.   source code documentation
> i.   Number of lines of source code for each component
> b.   build dynamics and system used for build (make)
> i.   Configuration Controls and Build Guides
> c.   runtime libraries (owned vs 3rd party)
> d.   QA, testing and diagnostic procedures and results
> e.   bug/support system
> f.   databases
> i.   ASP, SAAS etc databases
> ii.   Client licenses
> iii.   Configuration
> iv.   Others
> g.   installation/training manuals
> h.   user/help documentation
> i.   customer/contact lists
> j.   software release documents

8. Digital Rights Management System

a.   Proprietary system (explain/describe system)

b.   3rd party usage

c.   other

9. License and Client billing systems

a.   Proprietary (explain/describe system)

b.   3rd party usage

c.   other

10. What other digital or physical assets would be required with the software technology as part of any sale of the software product (project) to be self sufficient. For example third-party software and development tools, computer systems and/or other equipment, manufacturing facilities, etc. not identified above?

a.   What other services would be required with the software (e.g., access to computer   systems, manufacturing or laboratory facilities, engineering support, training time, etc.)?

11. Has any open source code been used in this software?

a.   Is there any intent to offer code, APIs, hooks for customer or open source modification?

12. Has this or any other "similar" types of software been licensed in or out?

a.   What were the terms of those license agreements (i.e., license revenue, scheduled payments, etc.)?

b.   Any such similar software (or any R&D-in-progress) been purchased?

c.   Has any of the software in question been acquired?

13. Technical contact(s) who would be the most intimately familiar with the software

a.   Development

       i.   Name, title
       ii.   Telephone number
       iii.   E-mail

b.   program/product management
       i.   Name, title
       ii.   Telephone number
       iii.   E-mail

c.   capabilities, and
       i.   Name, title
       ii.   Telephone number
       iii.   E-mail

d.   marketing
       i.   Name, title
       ii.   Telephone number
       iii.   E-mail

Exhibit H

An article about the beginning of Software Escrow by Gary B Watzke, Vice President and General Counsel for Iron Mountain Incorporated

In the late 1970s, computers were still a relatively new phenomenon, and software companies were just starting to come on the scene. The practice of licensing software instead of selling it outright was a new business model that was being tried by various vendors. During this time, a man named Dwight Olson worked for Control Data Corporation as a software product manager responsible for technology procurement. To support a project that he was working on, he contracted some software development work to an outside firm for $1 million. Unfortunately for Olson and Control Data, that firm went bankrupt. Olson never received his software code or the return of his company's $1 million. Try explaining that predicament to your CEO.

This story does have a happy ending, though. Olson realized that, in this new software industry, there had to be a way to protect software source code that would benefit both the software developer and the licensee. Olson founded Data Securities International in 1982, and technology escrow began. Before technology escrow was created, companies concerned about protecting the software that they acquired from developers sometimes stored software source code in a bank vault, the way that people might store their wills and the deeds to their homes. There were no specific requirements or processes connected to this type of storage, however, and no legal contracts were involved. Companies were at risk for loss of the stored software like any other bank customer.

During the first five years of his company's life, Olson says, "There was a need, but there wasn't yet a market" for technology escrow—in other words, software users hadn't yet realized the risks of the then-popular storage methods. Olson spent those years "preaching the gospel" and educating both software developers and businesses that used software applications about the need for technology escrow.

After a while, people started listening.

About the author, Dwight C. Olson, CLP emeritus

Dwight Olson is a Certified Licensing Professional (CLP), Director IP Licensing at EXEN Technologies, a Sr. Software IP Advisor to IP Metrics, and a Business Advisor at CONNECT. Olson was a founder of Data Securities International (DSI), which was acquired in 1997 by Iron Mountain Inc. He began his career in the research and development of supercomputers, parallel processing systems and related application architectures in the 60's and 70's. Prior to founding Data Securities International he was a software programmer, architect, researcher, product manager, product line manager, entrepreneur and has held many C level positions and board positions at software companies.

Mr. Olson is a past President of the Certified Licensing Professionals, Inc, a former President of the Licensing Executives Society (LES) USA and Canada and served as chair of the Licensing Executives Society International (LESI) IP valuation committee. As an international delegate to LESI he served as a voting member in the Intellectual Property Constituency (IPC) of ICANN. He was an associate member of the American Bar Association's Electronic Commerce Law and Information Security Committee working on the ABA's Digital Signature Guidelines.

Dwight Olson has over 40 years of experience in computer software commercialization. He is called the "father of technology escrow" and writes and speaks on the topics of technology escrow as a business tool, valuation of software, trusted third parties in licensing, IP, and about securities firms using only electronic records. Mr. Olson received a bachelor's degree in mathematics and teaching credentials from Augsburg University.

Books: "Northern Lights the Beauty of the Forgotten Scandinavian Enamel Jewelry Artisans" ISBN-13: 978-0-578-44439-0